GHOSTS OF WAR

[THE TRUE STORY OF A 19-YEAR-OLD GI]

GHOSTS OF WAR

[THE TRUE STORY OF A 19-YEAR-OLD GI]

RYAN SMITHSON

Collins
An Imprint of HarperCollins*Publishers*

Collins is an imprint of HarperCollins Publishers.

Ghosts of War: The True Story of a 19-Year-Old GI
Copyright © 2009 by Ryan Smithson

 Library of Congress Cataloging-in-Publication Data
Smithson, Ryan.
 Ghosts of war : the true story of a 19-year-old GI /
Ryan Smithson.
  p. cm.
 Includes bibliographical references and index.
 ISBN 978-0-06-166468-7 (trade bdg. : alk. paper)
 ISBN 978-0-06-166470-0 (lbr bdg. : alk. paper)
 1. Iraq War, 2003– —Personal narratives, American—
Juvenile literature. 2. Smithson, Ryan—Juvenile
literature. 3. Soldiers—United States—Biography—
Juvenile literature. I. Title.
DS79.76.S6225 2009   2008035420
956.7044'373—dc22   CIP
                                          AC

Typography by Jennifer Heuer
09 10 11 12 13 CG/RRDB   10 9 8 7 6 5 4 3 2 1
❖
First Edition

For
SGT James H. Conklin
and
EQ Platoon

This is a work of nonfiction, and although some names and identities have been changed in order to protect the anonymity and privacy of the individuals involved, the events contained herein are all true. They have been faithfully rendered as I have remembered them, to the best of my ability. Though details come from my keen recollection of such, they are not written to represent word-for-word documentation; rather, I've retold them in a way that evokes the true feeling and meaning of what happened. All of the following stories are written to reflect the essence of the mood and spirit of my experiences as I lived them and to portray the individual personalities of my fellow soldiers.

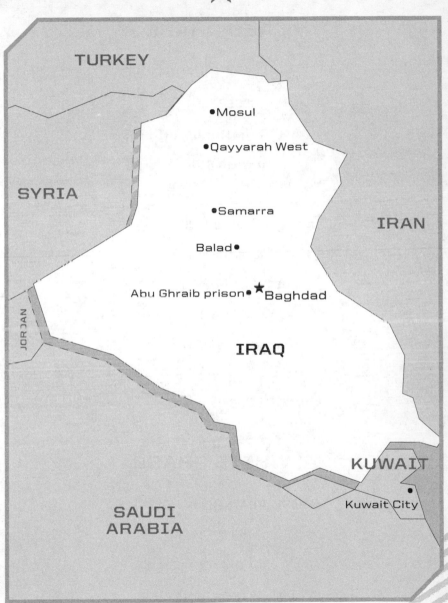

PART III
///////// **BLUE PHASE** /////////

GHOSTS OF WAR

[THE TRUE STORY OF A 19-YEAR-OLD GI]

PART I
//////// RED PHASE ////////

///////// STUCK IN THE FENCE /////////

East Greenbush, New York, is a suburb of Albany. Middle-class and about as average as it gets. The work was steady, the incomes were suitable, and the kids at Columbia High School were wannabes. They wanted to be rich. They wanted to be hot. They wanted to be tough. They wanted to be too cool for the kids who wanted to be rich, hot, and tough.

Picture me: the average teenage boy. Blond hair and blue eyes, smaller than average build, and I'll admit, a little dorky. I sat in third-period lunch with friends wearing my brand-new Aéropostale T-shirt and backward hat, wanting to be self-confident. The smells of greasy school lunches filled the air. We were at one of the identical fold-out tables. We were talking, but my thoughts were on my girlfriend, Heather. She was a senior this year and would finally be done. I was a junior and had two more years to go. What a drag.

I had turned sixteen less than a month ago, and so far being sixteen was boring as hell. I remembered watching shows like *Saved by the Bell* and *Welcome Freshmen* when I was a kid. How amazingly cool high school had seemed in those shows.

I remembered coming to the high school in fifth grade for a district-wide band concert. I marveled at these independent creatures who had their own cars and girlfriends and after-school jobs and holes in their jeans. They were free in the truest sense of the word.

And then, overnight it seemed, I was sitting in Columbia doing all the "independent" and "wild" things that teenagers did. What a joke. High school was so typical and predictable. Everyone here was so occupied with discovering the definition of cool.

To some, cool was Abercrombie and popped collars. Some thought cool was playing sports. Some thought cool was drinking before the homecoming dance. And others swore that cool was not trying to be cool: nonconformists with black nail polish, leather boots, and oversized safety pins in their ears.

Our free expression was in so many ways just a

restriction of our identities. All of us trying to be something we weren't. Even the nonconformists were conforming.

High school, I guessed, was just a chapter, something standing in the way of real freedom. High school didn't even seem real. It seemed so fake.

A friend of mine came into the cafeteria and sat down next to me.

"You hear?" he asked us.

"What?"

"A plane crashed into the World Trade Center."

"That sucks," I said.

The conversation picked back up and we talked about sex or drugs or something equally as interesting. It wasn't that we didn't care about the Trade Center. We shook it off as an accident. We assumed some drunk or stupid pilot had misjudged, clipped a wing, or something, and we shook it off. Shit happens.

The bell rang and the hallways exploded with raucous, horny teenagers. I visited Heather in the hallway, walked her to her class, and went to fourth period, Trigonometry. My math teacher, being pretty obsessive-compulsive, said that we weren't going to watch CNN all period. We were going to learn trig. She mentioned something about the crash but quickly moved on to the isosceles triangle. None of us realized the magnitude of it all yet. Otherwise we would have watched CNN all period.

It wasn't until fifth period, American History, that I understood what happened. During math class, the second plane had crashed, and I walked into History to see a TV showing the now infamous news footage: two enormous twin towers that smoked from their tops, one plume a bit higher than the other.

I walked to my seat and sat down, eyes never leaving the television. I took off my hat, but I didn't open my notebook. I didn't take out my pencil or assume the slumped note-taking position. I knew we weren't going to be taking notes in American History class that day.

The class was abnormally silent. It was high school, and things were usually done in a loud, disrespectful manner. Our teacher, Mr. Barret, motioned to the television and said something I'll never forget.

"You guys are living history."

I never thought of myself as living history before 9/11. History was something that had already happened, something I studied in school. It came out of a textbook. It was hearsay, not real enough to count.

My mind tried to tell me I was watching a movie. It was on TV, after all, and everyone knows you can't believe everything you see on TV. We watched in horror as the first tower collapsed into itself like it was being demolished. This was real, terrifyingly real. The sort of real that makes you lose hope. The atypical, unpredictable kind of real that you never see coming.

That night I called Heather and we talked for a long time about how shocking the attacks were.

"This is probably how people felt after Pearl Harbor," said Heather.

"Probably," I said. "Makes you realize some things."

"Like how crazy the world can be," she said. "It's scary. This is going to cause a war."

"I know."

The next day at school Heather told me she'd had a dream we were attacked. Right in Albany, she said. You could see the city exploding from Denny's, where we worked. Since then, once in a while, she had these dreams. They were always different scenarios related to terrorism, but we were always together . .

"They feel like the world is ending," she said about the dreams.

But, contrary to her dreams, life went on. Wrestling season started and was filled with all the hard work, sweat, and pain of my first two seasons.

On nights and weekends I continued working at Denny's as a dishwasher. And Heather worked as a server.

Heather and I broke up, dated other people, and got back together. Then we broke up again, dated more people, and took a final vow to give it one more shot.

As the fall approached, I dreaded going back to school. Not only did I have to finish a whole other year of high school, but senior year inevitably meant making all the decisions about the future.

For me, the future was a complete paradox. On one hand colleges were virtually throwing themselves at me through my mailbox and teachers were pushing that "know what you want to do for the rest of your life" attitude. Yet, on the other hand I wanted to stay a kid. Parents and teachers were so intimidating when they talked about the "real world" and taxes and mortgages and bills and insurance. With freedom comes responsibility and I wasn't sure if I was ready for all that.

Teens want to know what they should do for the rest of their lives. But how can people with no life experience outside of their crappy after-school jobs and awkward, hormone-induced dating life know what they're supposed to do in adulthood?

I didn't have any kind of plan. I longed for a purpose.

The more I agonized, the more I realized that what I'd watched in History class a year before was my purpose.

I'd thought about joining the military the moment I saw the towers fall, but I was too young. The military wouldn't take you unless you were seventeen. So after waiting a year, thinking it over, and feeling the increasing pressure of finding a purpose in life, I started talking to recruiters.

My family and friends were apprehensive when I told them I planned on enlisting in the service. My mother especially. She wanted me to go to college. She wanted me to pursue writing.

"I have to do this," I told her.

I'd heard all about September 11th. I'd watched it happen on television. I'd heard the theories and discussions about foreign policy that were way over my head. I'd bowed my head during tributes and moments of silence. I knew all about 9/11, but I felt like it was my generation's responsibility to do something about it.

One night I invited an army recruiter to the house before dinner. I told him my situation, the reasons I wanted to join. My mom and dad stood off to the side as the recruiter recommended the reserves.

"It's one weekend a month and two weeks a year," he said. "You can still go to college. You can still have a job outside the military. And they'll only deploy you if they need you."

Keep in mind that this was only the fall of 2002. The war hadn't started yet.

I discussed everything with my parents.

"If you're really going to do this, I think you should join the reserves," my mother said immediately.

"I figured," I said.

"Do whatever you think is right, Ryan," my father said.

"Yeah," I said.

"The reserves probably is the best option," he added. "You

still get to go to college. Plus, what if you end up hating the military? If you go full-time, there'll be no escape."

"That's true," I said.

There was a pause.

My dad repeated, "Do whatever you think is right."

Wrestling season started in November, and it was going to be my best year. I could feel it. I had been going to the wrestling club almost every chance I got. My balance had improved, my takedowns were flawless, and my mat sense was so confident that I could practically wrestle with my eyes closed. Everything changed during our first match.

While I took a shot on my opponent, my left kneecap decided it wanted to relocate to the outside of my leg. The ensuing injury kept me out for a third of the season.

Watching my teammates from the bench, I thought of 9/11. It had changed my entire worldview. I thought parents and teachers were intimidating when they talked about the "real world." But I was in the real world. In New York City, three hours away, people crashed planes to kill other people. And my knee had ruined what felt like my last chance for accomplishment.

Life was not typical or predictable. And I learned even life in high school was no different. I couldn't change my knee injury, but I still had lots of control over my future.

My country had been attacked. My people had been

attacked. Enlisting, volunteering, giving oneself for the greater good: that's what you're supposed to do in this situation. So I did it.

In December I went to the MEPS (Military Entrance Processing Station) in Albany. I took the eye test, the hearing test, and all the other physical tests. My knee hurt only when the doctor made me do the duck walk, a squatted walking exercise. But I toughed through it and was fine. After the physical I took the army multiple-choice test, called the ASVAB (Armed Services Vocational Aptitude Battery), and chose the job I wanted, my MOS (Military Occupation Specialty). I decided to become a Heavy Construction Equipment Operator, or a 21E (Twenty-one Echo). As a 21E I would learn how to operate bulldozers, scoop loaders, dump trucks, road graders, and scrapers so the army could use me for whatever the army needed to do with bulldozers, scoop loaders, dump trucks, road graders, and scrapers. Assuming I made it through nine weeks of BCT (Basic Combat Training), I would learn my MOS at an additional nine weeks of AIT (Advanced Individual Training). I'd conduct both trainings at Fort Leonard Wood, Missouri.

It's funny how the army talks, this whole other language of acronyms and jargon. It may seem impossible to someone who isn't familiar with it, but recruits just pick it up along the way. Think of it as on-the-job training. On only my first day I was barely allowed to call myself a recruit, yet I already knew what MEPS, ASVAB, MOS, BCT, and AIT meant. Plus, I knew that E was for Echo.

In the military every letter corresponds to a word. All the cool conversations you hear in movies about Alpha team and Delta this and Foxtrot that, it's all real terminology based on the phonetic alphabet. Over a radio an "E" could sound like a "D," or an "O" could sound like a "no," and in military operations where precision is everything one misheard digit could mean people's lives.

Now, there are two ways to sign up for the military: as an officer or as an enlisted soldier. To be commissioned as an officer a recruit has to have at least a bachelor's degree, so I couldn't go that route even if I wanted to. Not that I wanted to. Officers are the soldiers who have to plan and run everything. When you hear of lieutenants, captains, majors, colonels, and generals, you're hearing about officers. But when you hear of privates, specialists, and sergeants, you're hearing about the enlisted.

Further, there are four branches of the military: army, air force, navy, and marines. And each branch has three components: active duty, reserves, and national guard. Each of these components serves a different purpose for the Department of Defense (DoD), the department of the federal government that oversees the military. The Iraq war has changed everything we know about how these three components work.

Active duty: the everyday soldier. The men and women who live on military posts. The military is their career. These are the first soldiers deployed to a combat zone when there is one.

Reserves: the weekend warrior. For one weekend per month, reserve soldiers meet at a reserve station and "drill." At drill reservists do what active duty soldiers do every day, which means they train. Also, there is a two-week, mandatory AT (Annual Training), usually in the summer. During AT most units travel. Sometimes they go overseas to places like Central America or Japan and sometimes they stay in the U.S.

When active duty soldiers are deployed to a combat zone, they leave vacant spots back at their home stations or the military posts at which they've been stationed in the U.S. Just because a war is going on doesn't mean that military operations stop back in the States. So the reserve soldiers take the active soldiers' spots until they come home.

National guard: the other weekend warrior. Their commitment is basically the same as the reserves. The major difference is that they're funded by state taxes, while the reserves are funded by federal taxes—so a national guard is activated by its state for natural or man-made disasters. All the men and women in army fatigues cleaning up after a hurricane or an ice storm or 9/11: they're the national guard.

At the MEPS station I enlisted in the army reserves.

On the phone Heather asked me, "You think you'll be sent over?"

"It's too early to tell," I said. "If an actual war comes out of this, they'll send the active duty guys first. I might have to go take their spot for a while in the U.S., but that should be it. And even if I do get sent to Iraq, I'll be doing construction. I won't be fighting."

"Yeah," she said. "I hope not."

"Don't worry about it yet. I still have to get through basic."

That night Heather dreamed that we were running from incoming missiles. I was wearing an army uniform.

As summer approached, the war in full swing, I began to second-guess my decision to join the army. I told myself I was doing what I had to do. Not to mention I had already signed up. There was no easy way out, short of desertion. And in a time of war desertion equals jail time.

When Heather asked me why I would join the army in a time of war, I shrugged my shoulders and told her it just seemed like the right thing to do.

"That's very admirable, Ryan," she'd say. "Stupid, but admirable."

"Hey!" I'd say back. And we'd laugh.

Admirable, stupid, or whatever it was, the decision was made. I'd be leaving for basic training soon. I still needed to figure out exactly what my enlistment meant. As time passed, I wasn't sure how the events of 9/11 really affected me.

I hadn't lost anyone in the attacks. I hadn't known those people who were murdered. I didn't know what the terrorists were trying to say or how their message directly affected me. So I found out.

During Labor Day weekend of 2003, a month before I was scheduled to leave for Fort Leonard Wood, Heather and I took a trip to New York City. I had lived in New York my entire life and never been to the City. I wanted to see the place, its magic and energy. And I wanted to see Ground Zero.

I needed a reminder.

We stayed in Manhattan and saw as many sights as we could in the three-day weekend. New York City truly lived up to the hype. It was alive like nothing I'd ever seen. Broadway was a brilliant strip of flashing lights and artistic billboards. Times Square, full of shoppers and camera-toting tourists, seemed too big to be real.

In New York the energy of people had a way of spreading. It was so contagious that even the panhandlers seemed glad to be panhandling (though I'm sure they weren't). This energy seemed to animate the city air.

Except in one spot the energy stood still.

It was nighttime, and the only light at Ground Zero came from portable construction spotlights that sat in the enormous gray crater. The light had a soft blue quality to it, deathly.

The worst part was the silence. No taxis or buses drove there. No excited tourists shopped or snapped pictures. As usual people were everywhere, but no one said a word.

The buildings surrounding Ground Zero were abandoned, their windows still broken and missing. Hundreds of jagged, ugly holes peering down at us. Holes where the soft blue light couldn't reach. These black voids, just empty reminders of the lives lost.

Heather and I walked up to the fence that closed off the gray-blue crater from the public. Stuck in the fence were wreaths and flowers and notes from children; framed photographs of people in uniform and loose photographs of people with their families, small photographs that once sat in fathers' wallets. Stuck in the fence were U.S. flags and banners proclaiming, "We will never forget." There were final good-byes from relatives who couldn't say it in person, pictures of angels drawn by heartbroken children—angels with sad faces and gray-blue tears.

Stuck in the fence was New York City. Stuck in the fence was the United States of America. There were white people and black people and Hispanic people and Asian people and Jewish people and Muslim people and Christian people and small people and fat people and baby people and human people.

Stuck in the fence was me.

I'd heard all about September 11th. But I didn't feel the weight of it until I saw the fence.

I didn't know these people. They were not my friends or family. I had never met them. Their existence before that day meant nothing to me. But at that moment their existence meant everything to me.

I let go. My throat tickled, my nose ran, and I cried. I shed tears I didn't deserve to shed. I was not entitled to tears but they came nonetheless. These tears for injustice, for impurity, for virtue, for love, for hate, for misunderstanding, for innocence, for guilt, for nothing, and for everything.

Heather looked at me and cried, too. We stood like that for a long time, not saying a word. Just crying. We didn't sob; it was respectful crying, like at a funeral. We held each other, and people walked around like ghosts.

A mother walked up to the fence, tears in her eyes, and dropped a fresh set of flowers next to a picture of a young man. She said something to the photograph and buried her face in her hands.

I felt trapped in rubble and the pressure was overwhelming. The Twin Towers didn't fall in Manhattan. They fell on me.

There is a certain romanticism that comes with being young. Young men and women just released from high school are ready to take on the world. They want to save it. They try for a while, but then they often get to a certain age and they give up. Because the world is a big place. It's impossible to fix, they think.

And that's the problem I saw. America had given up. And that's why the World Trade Center was allowed to fall.

If I don't do something, who will? I thought.

I stopped crying.

A month later I left for basic training.

///////// **RECEPTION** /////////

The army makes recruits stay at a hotel the night before they fly to basic training. This is to ensure a timely arrival for their flight (and no deserters). Among the dozen or so other recruits saying goodbye to their families, mine stands across from me. Heather has to work, so she can't be here. Last night, she gave me a kiss, told me she'd be waiting. In the lobby my father shakes my hand and hugs me like a man. My mother gives me a kiss and hugs me like her baby. My little sister, Regan, gives me a kiss, tells me to be strong.

They tell me they're proud of me. I say, "Okay."

They tell me to call or write as soon as I can. I say, "Okay."

"I'll miss you. I love you," we say.

I find my room. I lay on the bed and wait until the four thirty wake-up call. Maybe I sleep.

At five A.M., a bus takes us to Albany International Airport, where we board a plane and say good-bye to life as we know it.

After landing in Missouri I am squeezed onto a bus with fifty other people, mostly teenagers like myself, from all over the U.S. Not much is said as the bus bounces along the highway from the airport to the army post. Some of us have books. Some have CD players. I don't have anything. I sit in my seat wondering what to expect. I wonder if the army will change me as much as everyone says.

Driving onto post, I notice how mundane all the buildings look. Everything is exactly the same: perfect rectangles made of brick sitting on perfectly mowed lawns with perfectly straight hedgerows. We stop at one of the large brick buildings, and my mind races with questions.

Will there be screaming drill sergeants?

Will I be able to handle myself?

Is everyone else as nervous as I am?

A young woman in army fatigues steps on the bus and tells us to get out our IDs and follow her. So far so good.

Is this a trick?

I wonder if the drill sergeants are waiting inside the building for us. Just waiting like snakes under brush. I stand up and follow the crowd.

When we get inside, the young woman tells us, "This is reception. You'll be here for one week."

Reception is a week of in-processing. There are drill sergeants walking around but only to keep us in line. A true drill sergeant thrashing is rare. Reception is the army jargon meaning "week-long basic training bureaucracy." It's where we do paperwork, get our uniforms, do more paperwork, get our hair cut, more paperwork, get our training gear, more paperwork, get a shot in our left arm, two shots in our right arm, blood drawn from the inside of our elbow, a tuberculosis test on our forearm, and a horrible injection in the top of our ass that bruises for three days.

We can't talk during reception. We are pieces of equipment on an assembly line. It sounds fast paced, but in reality reception is very slow. There are a lot of recruits to in-process, and waiting is how we spend most of our time. So, as we wait to do more paperwork or wait for our next meal or for our next inoculation, we read our Smart Books.

The Smart Book is a two-inch-thick army manual we carry in our cargo pockets. It contains all the necessary knowledge a recruit must know in order to graduate from basic training. It has everything from the army's rank structure to proper marching technique to clearing a weapon's jam to the phonetic alphabet. If our Smart Book is not on our person, we might as well have forgotten to wear pants. To witness a true drill sergeant thrashing, just forget your Smart Book.

Reception: picture rooms with white concrete blocks for walls and green tiled floors. There is a horde of greasy high school graduates with all the hair cut off their heads. Half of them are standing in line waiting to enter a processing room. The other half are sitting on benches waiting to wait in the line that's waiting to enter another room, only to come out and wait some more. All these teens are dressed in the same green-tan-and-black camouflage, wearing the same shiny black boots. Their bald heads are buried in the same gray, spiral-bound army manuals.

Even when there's free time, when we get back to our enormous sleeping bay and can relax and read a book or write a letter home, it feels like waiting. The bay is filled with bunk beds and wall lockers and snoring men. And every night, two or three times a night, the fluorescent lights flip on and dozens of new recruits wash in and join the party. So even sleeping is like waiting, waiting for the next set of nervous teens to wake us up and fumble around on their squeaky mattresses.

If this isn't the longest week of my life, then kill me now. With each day the anticipation for basic training grows until it feels like a whitehead ready to explode. Each day feels like the end will never come. I haven't even started basic training and I already want to quit, to tell the army to shove that stupid Book up its ass. I don't feel any Smarter.

Finally, the last day of reception arrives. I pack all my gear into a green duffel bag and meet the rest of the company in front of the barracks. A company is a group of about two hundred soldiers. Our newly issued military IDs and our dog tags are checked, and then we're stuffed into cattle-carrying cars.

The line progresses as one cattle car fills up. The giant sliding door rattles shut, and the truck pulling the cattle car drives off. A second one fills, closes, and leaves. And a third. I step onto the fourth. When everyone is loaded, the door slides shut and the cattle car takes off. Sardines aren't packed this close.

Except for the bouncing and squeaking, the ride is long and silent. The inside is dark, shielded. There are no windows (the army doesn't want us to know our way back), but there are small holes near the roof. Breathing holes so the cattle don't suffocate. Sunlight shines through these holes, casting dusty rays across our paralyzed faces stuck like dents in ice cubes. Too scared to melt.

Somewhere there are angry drill sergeants just waiting for us to unload. I can feel my heartbeat in my throat, and I wonder if this is what it's like on the way to a combat zone.

We know we're approaching our new barracks when we hear the muffled booms of drill sergeants screaming at those privates who've already stopped and unloaded. Our brakes squeal. The cattle car stops. We look at one another, wondering if we're supposed to get out or if we're supposed to be let out. We've spent a week waiting, waiting to be told what to do and where to go. So we wait.

The rattling door flies open, showering us in sunlight, and three drill sergeants demand to know just what the hell we are waiting for. There is a mad rush, and my brand-new combat boots don't even touch the ground before a drill sergeant is in my face. The brim of his "brown and round" hat pecks at my nose.

"Why are you touching my hat, private!" he screams, veins throbbing.

"Sorry, Drill Sergeant," I say.

"Oh, so I'm a sorry Drill Sergeant?"

"No, Drill Sergeant."

"Don't you ever tell me no, private!"

"Yes, Drill Sergeant."

The scene is chaos. Panicky privates run around like cockroaches when the kitchen light turns on. Drill sergeants are the feet trying to stomp at them.

Move Faster! Stand Here! Run There! Find a Spot in Formation! Get Moving! Faster! Shut Up!

"Yes, Drill Sergeant."

"I said, 'Shut Up!'"

The first smell of basic training is humid rubber. That's The Pit.

The Pit is a depression the size of a football field stuck between four brick barracks—four companies of privates learning to become soldiers. We are the newest of the four companies and we run around like the lost, scared wannabe soldiers that we are. The Pit smells like rubber because it's filled with chopped tire pieces. It is soft and squishy and vile. The army's recycling program.

I take my place in The Pit as part of a wide formation: fifteen feet between each private. The shouts of the drill sergeants echo off the four surrounding barracks, and the resulting sound is an avalanche. I stand and listen to one drill sergeant up front with a megaphone, trying to shut out the roars of a dozen other drill sergeants coming from all directions. The drill sergeant with the megaphone yells at us, tells us all about the position of attention, and another screams in my face because I'm not doing it right.

They tell us we're worthless, that mommy ain't here, and that we are no different than any other rotting piece of compost in army fatigues. They tell us we're not wanted, that our recruiters lied to us, and that we should just go home. And the privates just stand there taking it as the drill sergeant with the megaphone tells us that our asses belong to him and that not even God Himself can save us now.

///// **BASIC TRAINING PART I** /////

Only after we have been completely destroyed can we begin to find ourselves.

The drill sergeants do it like this: they break us down, build us up, break us down again, and then build us back up. The first breakdown is the hardest part. It's the first three weeks, and they call it Red Phase.

After a while push-ups and Red Phase have the same meaning. Sometimes we do them in cadence.

Drill sergeant yells, "One, two, three . . ."

We yell, "One."

"One, two, three . . ."

"Two."

One is down, two is up, three is down, the count is up.

This way, one count means two push-ups. Two counts mean four. Thirty-five means seventy.

Other times, when the drill sergeants want to be extra mean, we do push-ups in half steps.

Drill sergeant yells, "Down . . ."

We yell, "Attention to detail."

"Up . . ."

"Work as a team."

And of course there's always a longer pause after "down" than there is after "up."

The army takes our clothes and gives us camouflage. To hide us. To hide who we are, who we were. All of us convicts in camouflage green jumpsuits. They take our designer shoes. They give us combat boots ("to be shined every night, private"). They take our sunglasses and give us patrol caps. They take our chewing gum. And the television, our CD players, and the lunch Mommy packed.

"'An Army of One,' my ass!" they yell. "You are not one. You are no one! You are battle buddies. Every one of you relies on every other."

They take it all. The drill sergeants strip us of every luxury, everything we've ever convinced ourselves to be a necessity. They take who we are and flatten it, everything we think we know about it. They take it away so all we're left with is each other and the hair on our chinny-chin-chins. Then they give us a razor blade and tell us to shave.

Sitting in the barbershop chair, we get the hair cut off our heads like dogs at the vet. We watch in the mirror as our identity floats to the ground. We watch as the barber sweeps it up, puts it in the trash. Right where it belongs. The hair of a hundred other recruits, a hundred other identities mixing and blending until they're all the same.

We're all the same.

The basic training barbershop smells like old sweat and mineral oil. A dark and vague smell, like a back alley full of hot metal. The mineral oil so the trimmers stay clean and efficient. The distilled stink of it mixing with skin and sweat. This smell, it's people losing their identities. It's boiling hot, bottled anger. It fills the barbershop and wafts through the silent line of camouflaged privates at parade rest.

Parade rest: a modified position of attention. Hands behind the back, clasped right over left, head and eyes forward, mouth shut, feet shoulder-width apart. Can't walk while you're at parade rest. When the line progresses, come to attention: snap the feet together, hands go to fists and drop to the sides. Step forward. Then back to parade rest.

The barbershop's efficiency can be seen from a mile. A line of privates in one side, two-week old fuzz atop their round heads; a line of privates out the other side, skinned and clean.

After our haircuts we form up by platoon. Fifty privates

in each platoon. Four platoons in the company. Standing in formation waiting for the rest of the company is how we do everything. A formation consists of four ranks: horizontal lines, privates standing shoulder to shoulder. In our ranks we "dress, right, dress." This means we are lined up perfectly with both the private to our right and the private to our front. This ensures that every private has a place and can be seen and accounted for at any given time. All a drill sergeant has to do is count the number of privates in the first rank and multiply by four.

The golden rule of a formation: never walk in front of one.

A private leaves the barbershop double timing, or running, just like he's supposed to. He pulls his camouflage patrol cap over his bald head and double times toward his platoon. He doesn't remember the golden rule. I want to yell, to tell him to think, but the second golden rule of a formation is you don't talk while standing in one.

As fast as lightning, a drill sergeant is in his face.

"You just want to run around disrespecting formations all day, do you?"

"No, Drill Sergeant!" yells the kid, snapping to parade rest.

"Now you're lying to me?"

"No, Drill Sergeant!"

"Well, which is it, buttercup? Did you just disrespect my

formation or did you just lie to me?"

Drill sergeants have such a knack for making simple situations complicated.

"I just meant—"

"You meant what? Now I'm the liar?"

"I—"

"I—I—uhh—" mocks the drill sergeant.

"I disrespected your formation, Drill Sergeant."

"Oh, a little integrity, I see. That's mighty kind of you. Tell me, Honest Abe, what are the other six army values?"

These can be found in the Smart Book.

"Drill Sergeant, the other six army values are loyalty, duty, respect, selfless service, honor, integrity—"

"Yeah, we covered that one!"

"Yes, Drill Sergeant. Um, uh, respect—"

"Said that!"

"Um . . . Drill Sergeant, I . . ."

"You what?"

"I—"

"You what? *You what?*" The drill sergeant screams in his face. "Well, cupcake, while you're stammering around trying to figure out that the seventh army value is *personal courage*, your battle buddy is over there dying from a bullet wound!"

"Yes, Drill Sergeant."

The kid looks like he wants to cry. No one is really dying

from a bullet wound. The drill sergeant is proving a point. In combat there's no time to think. You just act.

"Cannon cockers until I say stop!"

Anywhere else the kid's punishment would have been called squat thrusts. In basic training they're called cannon cockers.

The kid stands at attention, drops his hands to the ground, and kicks his feet out behind him. This puts him in a push-up position. He pulls his feet back underneath himself and stands back at attention.

"One cannon cocker," he says.

"You forgot to say 'boom,' sweetheart!" roars the drill sergeant. "Do it right or they all do it."

He points to us. With his finger he's saying, "If one soldier makes a mistake in combat, they all suffer."

Kid drops, throws back his feet, and then stands back up.

"Boom!" he says.

"Damn it, private! You ride the short bus? Every time you kick your little feet, you say 'boom.' That's the cannon cocker. When you stand up, you say the count. Think you can handle that, numbnuts?"

"Yes, Drill Sergeant."

Drops to his hands. Feet shoot back like the recoil of the M16's buffer spring.

"Boom," he says. A hundred recruits watch him, hearing

his Mississippi accent echoing. Stand up. "One cannon cocker!"

Back down. His feet shoot out twice. "Boom. Boom."

Back up. "Two cannon cockers."

"Boom. Boom. Boom."

"Three cannon cockers."

This goes on for way too long. His booms the only sound. At the seventh cannon cocker, someone in the formation can no longer take the echoing Mississippian accent of this kid: "Baoum . . . baoum . . . baoum . . ."

"You wanna laugh at him, you little puke?" yells another drill sergeant. "You can join him!"

Now there are two. And they're both nervous and hysterical. They can't synchronize.

"Boom, boom, boom, boom, boom . . ."

"Baoum, baoum, baoum, baoum, baoum . . ."

Which gets them yelled at some more.

The rest of the shaved recruits form up, and we thank God that this cannon cocker charade is over. We are all seconds away from doing them. We stand there, a sea of bald boys learning to become soldiers one cannon cocker at a time.

Many people can't do it. Most of the privates who "wash out," or fail to complete basic training, do so during Red Phase. And the army doesn't care. It doesn't want the washouts. The army doesn't believe in pity, because its enemies don't believe in pity.

Only after we have been completely destroyed can we begin to find ourselves.

Red Phase is about reflection. It's about looking around and realizing how much all this means. This ground, this place we call a home. This space and time given to us for free. These people we call countrymen.

And the way it feels to lose it all, to lose our free will. The drill sergeants tell us when to train, when to push, and when to pull. When to laugh (never) and when to cry (don't even think about it). They tell us how to walk and how to talk, how to sit and how to eat, and when to shower and when to shit.

When we have something to say, we stand at the position of attention and request permission to speak. And hope the drill sergeant doesn't rip our bloody head off for interrupting his busy day.

Red Phase is about duty. The opposite of freedom.

And standing there being screamed at for not tucking in the corners of my bed sheets properly, I have an epiphany. The drill sergeant is two seconds away from tossing my whole mattress on the floor. He's five seconds from tossing my battle buddy's mattress on the floor. If we don't pick them up and remake our bunks in time, the whole room—six other privates' mattresses—will be tossed. But it's okay. I get it.

If you sacrifice your freedom, you'll learn what freedom means. And once you know what freedom means, you'll know why it's worth fighting for.

Sacrifice. Godforsaken, selfless, nothing-matters-less-than-my-well-being sacrifice. "I serve the country" is tattooed right across my forehead. I am a part of the all-warrior circus. We are snarling clowns with spiked teeth and bleeding gums. We smell like rotten war paint.

We smell like old camping gear. That's the smell of the army.

Mostly it's the TA-50, our field issue. The web gear that wraps around my chest like a python, its ammo pouches are full of the army smell. The Kevlar helmet that dents the top of my head smells like it's leaking army-scented oil. The rucksack, poncho, and the worn-out, recycled wet weather gear that doesn't work. That's TA-50, all of it reeking of the army.

That smell was stuffed into my duffel bag, inside my extra uniforms, my socks, and my brown underwear. (Yes, the army even tells recruits what kind of underwear they'll wear in basic training.) All of us, we smell like the army now, too. That smell is in the towels we use to dry off. It's in the sheets we sleep in. It's in our washcloths and wall lockers and brown T-shirts. It has been said that after a certain amount of time, one can get used to any smell. That's either not true or I need more time.

The army smell is distinct, something I'll smell a thousand years from now in my hundredth next life and I'll turn and say, "That's a smell from a previous life, A.D. 2003." The army smell is indestructible. It cannot be washed off or worn out. It cannot be manipulated or covered up with cologne or deodorant. It is pungent but hardly offensive. It's earthly, the army smell, like dust on a shelf. It's ancient fabric dipped in OD (Olive Drab) green dye and handed out to new recruits.

Sometimes you can rub at the new dye and it lightens. It fades away little by little. Then if you look hard enough, the old dye peeks through. Behind the ugly green-brown dye, the fabric is blue. Some of the spaces between the splintering olive color, the parts that were given up, sacrificed, these parts are white. In some spots the old fabric is stained and bloody. Red.

Lying in my bunk writing a letter to my parents, the red flashlight making my paper pink, I realize that when I am sent to the Sandbox like all the drill sergeants say I will be, if I die, the flag they give my parents, the Stars and Stripes, is going to smell like the army. Dipped in new dye, sure. Crisp and clean and folded in a compact triangle, absolutely. But it'll still smell like the olive green and dirty brown of everything that surrounds me here in basic training. It will smell like these sheets. And whenever my parents remember their son, they'll have to smell that old vinyl, dust-on-a-shelf smell I now live in.

I try not to think about it. I finish my letter and lay my head on my pillow, thinking of tomorrow, Sunday.

Sunday is our day off but that doesn't mean what you probably think. We don't get to talk to our families, run down to the PX (Post Exchange) to buy a soda, or take a leisurely walk around post. Our heads are still shaved, the drill sergeants still yell, we still crawl out of our racks at four thirty A.M., still wear army greens, and still get three minutes to hammer chow. The difference is that there is no training.

During the week we practice marching. We do teamwork-building exercises and confidence courses, the obstacle courses for which basic training is famous. We do hand-to-hand combat and pugle stick fighting. We sit through classes on the army values, first aid, and financial skills. We walk through a gas chamber full of CS gas, the tear gas that police use at riots. All this stuff is training. And all of it comes to a halt on Sunday.

Sunday is the only day we can look forward to each week. In drill sergeant language our only task on Sunday is to "conduct barracks maintenance." This means clean.

Using pine oil almost exclusively, we scrub every inch of our section of the barracks. On our hand and knee. We buff the floors, scour the sinks, polish the toilets, scrub the showers, and wipe the counters. (Regular shaving cream gets a shoe scuff off a tile floor like no one's business.)

And the smell, that virtuous smell of Sunday. Tangy and sour, like pine pitch fermented in peroxide wrapped in sin. Are sins really forgiven on Sunday morning? Or are they just washed up and sanitized, covered up with a piney solution?

The mixture of pine oil and sin, it smells like atheism.

After one brave soul announces to the drill sergeant that we are done cleaning, he comes upstairs with a white glove and runs his finger along the windowsills, wall lockers, radiators, shower walls, and everywhere else. If he sees a speck of dust, it's back to cleaning.

During the first Sunday of Red Phase, we're thinking if we clean quickly, we'll have time to make a phone call or more leisure time. We soon find out how naïve we are. Even if the drill sergeant doesn't find dust, he finds dust. And since we bothered him before the job was done, we are irrevocably stupid and therefore deserving of some good old-fashioned PT (Physical Training). We quickly learn to use the entire Sunday to clean.

But cleaning is the facade. Sundays are about escape. We can talk to one another all day on Sunday. We are finally allowed to find out about one another. I would not usually be interested in what fifty people, whom I met only weeks ago, would have to share with me. But here it seems important. For some reason basic training makes me appreciate strangers.

And Sundays are about getting away. Sundays give us an excuse to leave the pine-scented barracks, if only for an hour. There are Protestant and Catholic services. There are Buddhist and Hindu services. There are Jewish and Muslim and Southern Gospel services.

As a bus rolls up for the first service of the day, the whole company forms up outside the barracks.

"This one's for you Methodists," yells the drill sergeant.

Only a few people step out of formation and board the bus.

"There better be more for the Protestant service," says the drill sergeants. "I don't want to look at you nasty privates all day."

And then there's the atheist. Born and raised in New York City.

"What if you don't believe in God, Drill Sergeant?" she asks from the back of the formation.

Now, there are a couple things that need to be understood here. First of all, just because Red Phase is almost over and White Phase starts tomorrow doesn't mean we're out of basic training. You can't just yell out in the middle of a formation. I'm not terribly religious myself. Spiritual, I'd say. But regardless. We're standing in the heart of the Bible Belt, sister. The majority of the military comes from the South, and if you think they don't love teaching valuable lessons to every blasphemous, Northern hippie they come across, you've got another think coming.

"What did you say?" he says, walking over to her spot in formation.

"I said, 'What if you don't believe in God, Drill Sergeant?'" she says.

We all wait to hear the drill sergeant yell "drop," meaning push-ups, or "front leaning rest position," meaning push-ups, or of course, "cannon cockers." But he says nothing. He pauses. A long time.

"There's no such thing as an atheist in a foxhole," he tells her.

I picture World War II and Vietnam flicks: soldiers sitting in foxholes praying with rosaries. This is how I make sense of what the drill sergeant told the atheist.

When you're in the shit and all you have are a rifle and your own ass, I think, *you'll turn to God.*

Sometimes God isn't listening. Pray all you want, and the only outcome you'll get is a lead slug through the forehead. But sometimes, just sometimes, God *is* listening. And God hates the bad guys, right? The reinforcements show up, and the Krauts or the Gooks are wiped out. The platoon survives against miraculous odds, and the American flag waves in the foreground. Roll credits.

I think, *Soldiers turn to God during war.*

///////////// MAYBE A RING? /////////////

After BCT I stay in Fort Leonard Wood for AIT and then finally return home in March 2004. The Iraq war has been going on for a year, and the military has captured Saddam Hussein.

Heather is in her last semester of college, about to get her Associate's degree, and still lives with her roommate in their apartment. As for *my* education, I'm now a full year behind the classmates of my graduating class. But I plan on starting community college in the fall. I guess I'll go for auto mechanics.

For now I continue working at the Denny's where I worked in high school. I am no longer a greasy dishwasher, though. I've moved up and become a greasy short order cook. It's decent work for being eighteen and living at home. And of course I spend the first weekend of every month at my reserve unit in Kingston, New York.

The unit is fairly new to me, even though I visited a few times before I shipped out. I don't know most of the soldiers, but I still have a feeling of camaraderie with them. I made it through basic training. I am their fellow soldier now. That's where the camaraderie comes from. People understanding and accepting you without your having to prove yourself.

As summer approaches, Heather and I move into an apartment in Troy together. I finally assume the responsibility of living on my own. The Real World isn't such a scary place after all.

Even though it's tiny and our neighbors are a little rude, this apartment serves as the foundation for the rest of our lives together. We talk over dinner. Mushy, romantic comedy stuff. Boyfriends talking to girlfriends about things they would never even consider talking about with their buddies. Things like "I missed you at work today, sweetie" and "Poor kitty has to get booster shots tomorrow" and "Which is a better aroma for our laundry, white lilac or summer breeze?" We talk of marriage and kids and owning a home. We talk of the future. We talk of the army.

"What happens if you get deployed?" Heather asks me.

I shrug.

"You think you will?"

"Yep," I say.

She nods slowly, bites her bottom lip.

"So . . ."

"So I'll pack my bags and give you a kiss."

"Maybe a ring?" she asks.

I smile and kiss her on the forehead.

"Maybe," I say.

Historically in peacetime our country's military is all volunteer. But the Iraq war is different. Now during wartime our country's military is still all volunteer. There hasn't been a draft. Problem is, there aren't enough active duty soldiers to function in Iraq and Afghanistan the way DoD needs them to. So the reserves and national guard are deployed.

I never really think it's coming. I deny the inevitability of deployment. I doubt the drill sergeants when they tell me I'll end up in the Sandbox sooner or later. I doubt myself when I tell Heather, "Yep, I'll be deployed." But my denial doesn't matter. Because duty comes first.

I am standing in the unit administrator's office when it happens. The UA picks up the phone. The guy on the other line asks a question and the UA repeats it.

"Is Private Smithson deployable?" he says.

To me he says, "Can you get your two oh one file out of that cabinet behind you?" and tosses me a key.

I turn around, unlock the filing cabinet drawer, and snatch my 201, my entire life history with everything from what hospital I was born in to my PT scores in basic training to what the MEPS doctor saw when he checked my asshole for hemorrhoids.

The UA flips through the thick folder, pulls out a typed sheet containing some secret, returns it, and hands me the file.

"Yes, he is," the UA tells the guy on the phone.

As I put the folder back, I say, "No. Tell them no." And I try to make it sound like I'm joking.

At least I finally have an answer to the question I've tried to answer since I enlisted. The million-dollar question, the first question people ask when they find out I'm in the military: "Will you have to go to Iraq?"

In my head the answer is usually, *Probably, jackass, and thanks for bringing it up.*

From my mouth, the answer that usually comes out is "Maybe."

People don't know what to say to this. They say, "Well, I hope not" or "Man, we shouldn't even be there," followed by a totally blank stare.

In the civilian world, it makes perfect sense: a deployment roster months ahead of schedule. But this is not the civilian world. This is the place where we are property of the U.S. government, and there is no such roster. There's no convenient, all-knowing inventory of names and social security numbers, all the soldiers who'll be deployed in the new year. And there is definitely not a neat little dotted line where one can write *I respectfully decline.*

People don't understand, and I don't bother explaining that I'll be lucky to get a full week's notice before I'm deployed. So when I respond to the million-dollar question, I press my lips together, nod my head, and say, "Maybe."

The phone call to my UA is from another engineering unit out of West Virginia. This reserve unit is just like mine here in New York. For one weekend a month and two weeks a year, the unit fills up with engineering soldiers and they train; they do their MOS. The way the army works . . . Well, I have no idea how the army works. But for this one soldier at this one moment during this one war, the way the army works is like this.

A general somewhere needs an engineering unit in Iraq. In one way or another he finds the unit in West Virginia. This reserve unit, like most others, is not at what the army calls "full strength," they have to pull soldiers from other units, oftentimes in other states. This is called "cross leveling." Hence the call to my unit administrator in New York.

The unit cross levels soldiers until it is at full strength and can therefore accomplish whatever mission it needs to do in Iraq. The unit ships off all its personnel and equipment to

Fort Bragg, North Carolina. This first stage of a combat tour is "mobilization training," and I'm sure there's an acronym for it.

So when I receive the call in September that I'm being deployed to Iraq, I don't enroll in college. I don't call my buddies for one last night on the town. I don't find some sleaze in a bar and take her home. I get on one knee and ask Heather to be my wife.

People ask me why I got married at nineteen. They think I must have knocked up some girlfriend. "Any kids?" is always their second question. People assume I'm just naïve. Or that my decision has something to do with money or car insurance, maybe tax breaks.

Really, the answer is none of the above.

See, a girlfriend means nothing to the army. Neither does a fiancée. Anyone other than your spouse or legal guardian may as well be your pet goldfish.

If anything happens to me while I'm deployed, unless that box for "next of kin" reads "Heather Smithson/Spouse," Heather won't get the phone call. She won't get the folded American flag. If I die in the next year, Heather would live her life saying she once had a boyfriend who died in the war.

Within two weeks we throw together a civil ceremony with a judge, a gown, two rings, flowers, a limo, cake, thirty friends and family members, and a reception at Buca di Beppo.

The future is unknown. And during the ceremony at Frear Park in Troy the fear of the unknown pervades. The wedding march playing on the portable radio is a rapid heartbeat. The roots of the flowers in the park are trembling. The warm September wind is icy mist on my neck. The pagoda overhead looms threateningly. Our families, frozen in this moment, are realizing that the promise being made today, this hello to our union, is in so many ways an elaborate good-bye. The whole situation, the way it's so sure of itself yet so unsure of everything else, is just a lavish ceremony to say, "I promise to be here if you come home."

///////////////// **EQ PLATOON** /////////////////

For two months I sit at home waiting for orders. I try calling. But when I'm told I'm calling too much, I stop calling. I'm given orders, but I'm not notified. And then I'm reported AWOL for not following them. It's all about bureaucracy.

I call the UA in West Virginia, and finally everything gets sorted out. My unit in Kingston promotes me from private to specialist before I leave to join my new unit at Fort Bragg, North Carolina, where they have started mobilization training.

Saying good-bye for basic training at Fort Leonard Wood was nerve-wracking. "Good luck, Ryan!" and "Do your best, pal!" Relatives smiling like I was about to be in a performance. Think of "Jingle Bells" at a fifth grade concert.

Saying good-bye for mobilization training at Fort Bragg is sickening. "I love you so much, Ryan" and "I'm so proud of you, pal." Relatives crying like I'm about to be in a war. Think of watching your own funeral.

My mom, dad, Regan, and Heather all cry like it's the last time they'll see me. "We'll see you when you get home," they say. The "when" for hope. No one says "if." But we're all thinking it.

I give Heather a final kiss and turn toward the gate. The tunnel is a throat, and it's swallowing me. I wave once more to my family. They hold each other, and I feel detached. They say they're proud, but I feel like I'm abandoning them. I walk down the tunnel, not looking back, and wipe my tears on my sleeve.

We land in Raleigh, North Carolina. I hate it already. My commander and the command sergeant major pick me up. The commander plans everything, and the sergeant major carries the plans out.

They make conversation with me in the car. I answer their questions but try to ignore them. The commander asks me if I'm hungry.

"No, sir," I lie.

Once we get to Fort Bragg, the sergeant major drives

us to Old Division Area: hundreds of identical, two-story buildings "dress, right, dressed" like soldiers standing in formation. These buildings were built during World War II for the soldiers being deployed then. I'm lonely but I feel a sense of loyalty to them, those old soldiers who'd gone through what I am going through now.

"You'll be part of equipment platoon," says the commander.

I get out of the backseat, grab my green duffel bag out of the trunk, and start toward the brown metal door. Nobody's around.

The rest of equipment platoon is out on an FTX (Field Training Exercise). A field training exercise is a war game. A unit stays in tents, observes noise and light discipline, and pulls security shifts all night long.

I dump off my stuff on an open bunk and take a self-guided tour. This barracks is two open bays stacked on top of each other. Each bay holds about two dozen metal bunk beds with a standing wall locker for each mattress. Everything's lined up (dress, right, dress) next to one another down either wall.

As I walk around, I think of the thousands of soldiers who have stayed here. Average GIs just like me, just waiting to go to war. None of them knew at the time whether or not their war meant anything. Vietnam, Korea, World War II. I wonder how many felt detached, scared. I haven't even been away from home for a whole day, and I already feel like the end of this combat tour will never come. I wonder about the soldiers who came before me.

Young soldiers like me. Boys getting yelled at for stubble on their chins, for not tucking in the laces of their boots. They smoke cigarettes the same way, for the same reasons. They talk about "back home" the same way, spit the same way when they recall a fistfight in high school. They puff their chests the same way when they talk about ex-girlfriends, laugh the same way when they brag about taking advantage of them.

And I feel connected with these anonymous soldiers, people I may have passed on the street a hundred times back home. Old men with scruffy beards who may have once slept in Old Division Area. People who may have felt the very same uneasiness as they dumped their belongings on an empty mattress.

I enter the bathroom and lean over the sink. In the mirror my eyes are desperate. There's a longing to be understood and accepted. To be strong and brave like I should be.

Soldiers seem so durable, so resilient, and so heroic in war novels. On the television screen they're afraid of nothing. I wonder if I have that same courage. Basic training is supposed to teach us bravery and fortitude. It's why,

I suppose, I was able to maintain my composure while boarding the plane for Bragg.

But courage also means being afraid, accepting a fear of the unknown. Anyone who claims to be unafraid as they sit in a barracks in-processing for war is either lying or crazy. And being crazy is not the same as being brave.

Bravery is being afraid of something but facing it anyway.

Life as I know it is over. For the next year or longer (my orders say eighteen months, but this is an intentional overestimate) my life is on hold. It's time to do my duty, to live up to my promise of service. It's time to abandon my family in the name of my country. Because that's what young men and women do when their country is attacked.

Suck it up, I tell my mirror self like a drill sergeant. *I'm not doing this for you.*

At dinner I have fried chicken and corn. I have powdered mashed potatoes and a hard roll. Then I walk home. The barracks. I'm already calling it home.

The platoon is back for the night, out of the field and eager for hot showers. Fifty kids from all over the U.S. Not all of them are kids, but most are under twenty-five. None of them have been to Iraq. They wash up, joke with one another, and introduce themselves to me.

The platoon sergeant—a short, stocky guy with a good sense of humor—finds me and shakes my hand.

"I'm Sergeant Munoz," he says.

Actually he's a sergeant first class. In the army we pretty much call every NCO (Noncommissioned Officer) "sergeant." To distinguish a newer NCO from an experienced one, we might say he's a "buck sergeant." This means he has three chevrons (pointy spikes on top of one another) and no rockers (the curved lines underneath).

A sergeant first class like Neil Munoz has three chevrons and two rockers.

Munoz recognizes the unit patch on my left shoulder. Turns out, Munoz and Struber, my squad leader back in Kingston, "went through the ranks together." In army lingo this means they were privates together, privates first class, specialists, and eventually sergeants. They grew up together.

A tall, clean-shaven man walks by. He looks young, maybe twenty-five, and seems to be in a hurry. I can see by the golden bar on his collar that he's an officer. This "butter bar," as the slang goes, means that he's a second lieutenant, the lowest rank of commissioned officers.

"I'm Lieutenant Zeltwanger, your platoon leader," he says, pronouncing the name written over his right breast pocket like "Zelt-wong-er." "Feel free to call me LT or LTZ. And of course, there's always the default. . . ."

"Yes, sir," I say.

He has a hearty laugh, this lieutenant.

"EQ platoon is a tight group. We take care of each other, even when this command doesn't."

He looks to the platoon sergeant, who's still standing next to me. Munoz smiles and nods.

"All right, sir," I say. "Thank you."

The lieutenant continues on.

The command sent EQ platoon out for an FTX with no tents or supplies. They promised to send out supplies, but after the platoon sat for hours in a rainstorm with nothing more than sleeping bags, the FTX was canceled.

I get down to Bragg, and the first thing my platoon leader tells me is that this command doesn't take care of us. This is only mobilization training. How will our unit get in and out of Iraq safely? Already, though, I am thankful to a part of EQ platoon. Already I am thanking God for Andy Zeltwanger and Neil Munoz.

There are four squads in the platoon. First and second are equipment operators. Third is the concrete squad. And fourth is the truck drivers. I'm one of the operators, and Sergeant First Class Renninger is my squad leader.

Munoz directs me out the side door of the barracks where Renninger's standing. At night any army post looks like this: identical buildings—each with one orange light in the exact same spot—old pine trees and about a million boot prints.

When I meet him, Renninger is standing outside the side door, taking in the scenery, smoking a Marlboro red. For the next year, when I need to find Renninger, he'll be standing outside a side door taking in the scenery, smoking a Marlboro red. Picture the rough guy in an old western movie only wearing desert camouflage and rubbing the stubble on his chin.

"I gotta shave," he says. "You meet the lieutenant yet, kid?"

"Yes, sergeant," I say.

"Great guy. Welcome to the family, kid. And don't you worry," he says, taking a final drag. "We'll take care of you."

He excuses himself and steps inside.

For the next couple of weeks I in-process for Iraq. Paperwork. Anxiety. It reminds me of enlisting: fill out this form, initial here, cover your right eye and read line three, sign here, dot this *I* cross this *T*. . . . Next.

The unit gives me an option of either rushing through in-processing or taking my time and meeting up with the unit overseas. Without question I tell them to rush me through. I already feel a connection with the platoon, and I don't need any more uncertainty.

After only a few weeks I see that EQ platoon is something you'd find only in the army. During wartime. With the exception of the four squad leaders, platoon sergeant, and lieutenant, we're fifty kids. We're sitting in this barracks swapping stories and getting to know one another. We're ignoring the fact that any one of us might not return home with the rest. We're acting as though nothing serious is on our minds, as if fear doesn't grip us every time the barracks' lights go out. As if we're not terrified every time we're left alone with our thoughts.

////////// **GI JOE SCHMO** //////////

We're a platoon full of simple GIs. We're not airborne Rangers or Special Forces or even Infantry. Hell, we're not even marines. We're army reservist engineers, and we have more invested in our lives outside than inside the military.

I am only one of these simple GIs, and I am nothing special. I am a copy of a copy of a copy. I'm that vague, illegible, pink sheet on the very bottom of carbon paper stacks. They will not make movies about me. There will be no video games revolving around my involvement in the war. When people write nonfiction books about the Iraq war, about the various battles and changes of command, I will not be in them. My unit will not be mentioned. We are not going to be part of any significant turning point in the war.

We're not going to bust down doors and search for weapons caches. We're construction. We're going to build crap. We're not going to hunt for insurgents. Our job is to stay away from the enemy. Our job is small, a minute part of the larger picture.

And I'm not even sure what this "larger picture" means. I'm not sure why we invaded Iraq.

I am just a GI. Nothing special. A kid doing my job. A veritable Joe Schmo of the masses, of my generation.

I am GI Joe Schmo.

I am one soldier, and I stand in one squad in one platoon in one company during the battalion formation. A squad is about twelve soldiers.

My squad, we're equipment operators. My platoon, we're equipment platoon. My company, we're headquarters company. The three other companies in the battalion—A (Alpha), B (Bravo), and C (Charlie)—are called "line companies." As headquarters company, we run the show. In Iraq we'll support the line companies. Plus, the commander tells us, we'll have our own missions.

EQ platoon is four twelve-soldier teams full of GI Joe Schmos. And we're in this together. Our wives and girlfriends are home. Our moms and dads and siblings left behind. All they have is one another.

All we have is one another.

And we're going to do whatever it takes to come home alive.

On December 1, 2004, the entire battalion packs into one giant plane. Our next stop is our refueling point in Germany.

I am flying over the Atlantic at night for the first time. No clouds, only light coming from the moon. A billion stars and moonlight dancing off waves that are thirty-seven thousand feet below me. There are no city lights. No streaks of red-and-white highway. There's no relation to anything in space, and zero relativity feels like zero gravity.

As I skip through time zones, I wonder how Heather's doing. She doesn't even know we're flying out today. Before we left the commander told us not to e-mail or call our families with information about dates and times. This is called OPSEC (Operational Security) and it's something the army takes very seriously. And for good reason.

In Iraq operational security matters more than anything, because any one intercepted message can jeopardize an entire mission and the lives of soldiers.

In all honesty this plane trip to Germany isn't that big of a deal as far as OPSEC is concerned, but I have to get used to it. And so does my family. So when I called them for the last time before we left the States, I told them,

"Soon. We're leaving soon."

OPSEC is for the better, but I still feel as if I'm abandoning my family.

After refueling in Germany we take off for our last stop: Kuwait. On a map of the world if the Persian Gulf is a mouth, Kuwait is the back of the throat. And when we're done in Kuwait, she'll swallow us, push us into the stomach. That violent, churning stomach.

We land near Kuwait City, the capital, and hop on a convoy of buses. Kuwait City is beautiful in a windy, flat, desert kind of way. I wish we were going there and not to some army camp in the middle of nowhere.

I am anxious, even though I'm not in a combat zone. Iraq is the dangerous country, the one that's always in the news, but I'm still anxious. Because the bus is bringing us into the unknown.

On the way to reception in basic training all I knew of it was the media image of loud, belittling drill sergeants. So that's what I expected.

On the way to some army camp in Kuwait all I know of the Middle East is the media image of car bombs and people rioting in the streets. So that's what I expect.

Looking out my window, I see a car passing our bus. A woman in the passenger seat holds up a thumb and smiles. Kids in the backseat see my uniform and wave. I don't wave back. I smile uncertainly.

It's nighttime, and there's not much of anything to look at once we get past the unique architecture of Kuwait City. Nothing to look at except for tough desert plants and trees that line parts of the edge of the road. I watch the empty desert go by, glad to see that it's filled with darkness and not car bombs or people rioting in the streets.

Munoz is sitting in front of me.

"It wasn't like this in the first Gulf War," he says.

"How was it?" I ask.

He pauses. "Different."

He tells me, "The Kuwaitis love the Americans now because we liberated their country in Operation Desert Storm in 'Ninety-one. But they weren't always so friendly. During the first Gulf War they were like the Iraqis are today. In another decade hopefully the Iraqis will appreciate us the way the Kuwaitis do."

Another car passes. The passengers wave to me. This time I wave back.

Munoz was an engineer in Desert Storm. Most of the time he ran a bulldozer. Twelve-hour shifts building long, large piles of dirt called berms to catch bullets.

My platoon sergeant had been a specialist like myself. He was a dozer operator, a GI Joe Schmo just doing his part. But it was a part of something bigger.

Maybe I'll be a part of an operation that changes an entire country. Kuwait is our stepping stone to Operations

Iraqi Freedom and Enduring Freedom for the country of Iraq.

How many people have an opportunity to change an entire country? How many people can find such a sense of purpose? How many people can say they did their small little part and the result was a whole country full of happier, free people?

Basic training taught me to appreciate freedom. My deployment, I hope, is allowing me to spread that freedom.

We get to Camp Virginia and unload our duffel bags. There are soldiers stationed here to in-process units like us. They take our IDs, for financial purposes, swipe them in a card reader, and give them back. They give us a briefing, but it's hard to listen. Traveling through eight time zones makes you real tired.

We split into company formations and get another briefing from our commander. He leads us to our group of tents. They're tan on the outside and white on the inside. They have wooden floors to prevent camel spiders and scorpions from crawling in our boots at night. It's December and the bugs aren't too bad. I notice it's chillier than I thought Kuwait would be. Low 40s at nighttime.

So far no car bombs, no scorpions, and no sweltering heat. With every new experience I learn how false my pretenses about the Middle East have been.

We stay in Kuwait for three weeks, getting used to the eight-hour difference in time zones and the foreign climate: the dry weather, the wind, the sand.

We are waiting for our engineering equipment (construction vehicles) to arrive on navy ships coming up the Persian Gulf.

PMCS (Preventative Maintenance Checks and Services) is an inventory and inspection of anything we use in the army—from our weapons to our gas masks to our engineering equipment. It's checking every nut and every bolt, every seal and every fluid level. And it's how engineers spend most of their time.

When there's nothing to do, we PMCS. After we're done, if there's still nothing to do, we PMCS. Before we use a piece of equipment, we PMCS. After we finish using a piece of equipment, we PMCS. It's such a common task that we joke about it. When we're caught sleeping, we tell our squad leader that we're PMCSing our eyelids. Renninger rarely finds it funny.

Another big part of our three weeks in Kuwait is to train on equipment. Every soldier in the platoon is cross-trained on the equipment we may have to operate during our tour. On an average day, between chow and cigarette breaks, first and second squad—the operators—cross-train the other squads on how to PMCS and use our loaders, dozers, hydraulic excavators, backhoes, Bobcats, and 5-ton dumps.

Then third squad—the concrete squad—cross-trains the other squads on how to PMCS and use their concrete mixing trucks, called PLSs. These are not the tumbling, cone-shaped tanks on wheels you see at construction sites. Picture some militant, OD green Willy Wonka machine that stores, mixes, and pours clay, limestone, and water. All of this is a very complicated process, too complicated for third squad to explain fully. So they give us a basic rundown of how a PLS works. Then a hands-on training driving the monster.

Fourth squad—the dump truck drivers—cross-trains the other squads on how to PMCS and operate the M916 tractors, the trailers that go with them, the 20-ton dump trucks, and the LMTVs (Light Medium Tactical Vehicles)—large cargo trucks each with a gun turret.

For almost every serious army training, we take steps—called the crawl, walk, and run stages. The crawling stage involves the PMCS and basic operation (i.e., how to turn it on). The walking stage involves driving around a cone, maybe on a civilian road, or in a Kuwaiti army camp, the military routes on camp. In the States running means you know what you're doing without really thinking. In Kuwait running means ready to do it in combat. Like anybody could ever be ready for combat.

After three weeks the commander announces that he wants the unit to be at its final destination by Christmas. None of us knows our final destination yet. All he can tell us is "It's in Iraq." *Gee, thanks.*

But we do know that Christmas is a blackout day. On a blackout day, other than routine patrols, convoys don't operate in Iraq. These Islamic assholes are on a holy mission, and they'd love to grease one of us on an international Christian holiday.

We spend our last week in Kuwait awake for hours and hours getting ready for the company-wide convoy. Half the company flew up to Iraq as the "advanced party," but there's still one hundred or more soldiers living out of duffel bags, sleeping on fold-out cots in tents, and organizing every piece of equipment headquarters company owns. PMCSing it, training on it, and trying to find a home for it in the massive convoy.

I'll be driving a 20-ton dump truck across the border into Iraq. I only know the 20-ton dump truck as far as crawl stage. I haven't operated it at all. I'm licensed on it, but I really haven't a clue how to drive it. And it's a stick shift.

Since we have so many soldiers to transport, standing in the back of my dump body will be four guys. One of them, Josh Miller, is in EQ's first squad with me. He'll be manning an M60 machine gun for which we'll have to weld a makeshift gun mount onto the dump. We'll be crossing the border of a combat zone. We'll be facing death.

LT organizes time for me to train on the 20-ton—a total of two times. My vehicle isn't the only one in need of armor and gun mounts, and when I'm done training with it, I park by the maintenance platoon.

The unit has stumbled upon quarter-inch thick plates of armor. It's weak, but it's better than nothing. And apparently it's made in the Middle East, because everyone calls it *haji* armor.

Maintenance platoon runs the extensive operation. They have the welding tools and oxyacetylene torches and bolts and power drills and grinders and air compressors and a hundred other things I never thought I'd be using at midnight in the Middle East. I get sleep in two-hour intervals every twelve to sixteen hours, and the entire company is working together to weld *haji* armor on as many trucks as possible.

Running on minimal sleep does things to a person. At first it's simply exhausting. I feel like I can no longer stand up or keep my eyes open. The pain in my leg muscles is deep and throbbing.

And my brain feels like it's on the verge of stopping completely. I have double vision. I wonder why our tent now smells like Grandma's basement, why my duffel bag smells like my father's aftershave.

As soldiers, we push ourselves. We push one another.

We're all in it together. If one quits, we all quit. So we keep one another from giving in to the sleep.

It's one o'clock in the morning, and the M916 tractor trailer to which I'm fastening armor is lit by a giant working lamp, just like the ones parked at construction sites back home and parked at Ground Zero, and it's powered by a generator that is low on gas; I'll have to fill it up soon. (I'm fastening a bolt and a nut.) *The 916's bumper number is H-1307, and it still needs a box of MREs and a little oil for the trip. Miller said he'll take care of that tomorrow, and he's a hard worker—grew up on a dairy farm in Ohio—so he'll do it. The truck's okay on water, but its left brake light is cracked a little. I wrote that up three days ago after morning chow: runny scrambled eggs like snot but awesome French toast.* (The bolt turns; the nut tightens.) *1307's missing an oil dipstick, which Sergeant Dodds, fourth squad's leader, said was okay as long as you cover the oil check with duct tape. He knows a lot about trucks because he's a truck driver back home. He once shot a hooker in the face with a fire extinguisher. See, the way fire extinguishers work is they suck the oxygen from the air, and since fire needs oxygen to burn, by sucking the oxygen you put out the fire, but a fire extinguisher in your face* (the bolt tightens) *sucks away the oxygen and makes you feel like drowning. And while this truck-stop hooker gasps for air, Arthur Dodds slams his driver side door shut and drives away, because he's married, has been for fifteen years, has two kids, the youngest of whom he nicknamed "Pickleman."* I notice a long shiny hair in the dust cloud off to my left, and (righty tighty, lefty loosy) *I quickly place that hair on the head of the only female in EQ platoon: SPC Alyssa Doudna. A pebble flies out from under her boot as she walks away from the group of welders, grinders, and me. The pebble's from the smoking area, and I wish such an attractive young woman wouldn't smoke.* (The thin armor gets closer to the door.) *I spot the oil stain on SPC Josh Roman's left desert combat boot. I laughed hysterically yesterday when he spilled hydraulic oil on himself while he was filling one of the scoop loaders, and now he's sitting on the wheel well of the front tire as he bolts armor to the door.* (His bolt tightens.) *And he's laughing at a story being told by SGT Buckelew, who stands behind me and who's being funny and witty because his expanded, sleep-deprived mind operates on a level that we're all addicted to like chocolate-covered crack, and he's telling us about this time in Sunday school when one of the nuns farted. She kept teaching like nothing had happened, and Wilfred Buckelew III, he held in his laugh forever before he burst out hysterically, and he was beaten across his hand with a ruler. Roman and I laugh hysterically because Buck's face and impression of himself trying to hold in a laugh is the funniest expression we've ever seen, and there's a maniacal quality in my laugh that I am very proud of.* (The bolt tightens fully and the armor is on the door.)

Our shift is over. We'd love some sleep, and none of us is very hungry. But we decide to walk a half mile to the chow hall anyway. The thing that's great about army camps overseas is they have four meals a day. Because so many soldiers are working through all hours of the night, there's a midnight chow. We fill the generator with gas first, and the three of us walk and talk and laugh and bond on a level I never thought possible with people I've known less than two months. We eat through our hour-long break and then continue working.

And this is the life of a soldier in Kuwait. Soldiers doing what they have to do to enter Iraq, a country they don't really want to visit in the first place. Simple GIs doing their part in their generation's war. Our involvement probably won't mean anything when the war's all said and done. The war will probably come to the same conclusion no matter what we do. So we do what we're told. There's no point in fighting it. Just do the best we can. Me and this ragtag group of GIs called Equipment Platoon.

The army tells me to go to Fort Bragg so I do it. The army tells me to pack my shit and hop a plane to the throat of the Persian Gulf so I do it. The army tells me, an average teenage boy just doing what he can after witnessing the worst attack on American soil since Pearl Harbor, to armor my own 20-ton and then drive four boys and a platoon sergeant into a combat zone so I do it.

///////// COLD LIGHTNING /////////

I'm not really ready for it. I'm a GI following orders. Somehow I think we'll be pulled back, our mission scratched. "Sorry about the confusion, folks. Return home to your families." But, really, no such luck.

It goes on as planned. Our convoy leaves for Iraq on December 22, 2004. And ready or not, here it comes.

Driving in the middle of a thirty-vehicle convoy, I feel my nerves relax. This is how training is supposed to work. You do it so much, it feels natural. True, this is my third time driving a 20-ton dump truck, but my MOS is operating equipment. I'm used to the rough, wide handling of military junk, and my experience relaxes me. Of course we're not yet in Iraq.

After a full six hours of convoying, we stop at another camp in Kuwait: Camp Cedar Two. There isn't enough room or necessity for us to be set up with tents like at Camp Virginia, so we stage the vehicles in a large formation and use them for a barracks.

Attached to my rucksack is the army-issue sleeping bag that smells like old vinyl and cooked pine. When we stop, the vehicles are staged in two long lines. I'm somewhere in the middle, and I dismount the tall dump truck to begin my after-operations PMCS.

As I come around the right side of the 20-ton, I see SGT Tim Folden doing an after-PMCS on his M916. He's rubbing his backside with his empty hand.

"How's your ass?" I ask.

"I'll let you know once I can feel it again," he says. We both laugh.

We continue our PMCS and then head off to dinner. In the chow hall I find one of the long tables with EQ members sitting at it. At this table the meal is quiet. Soldiers stationed at this camp surround us, and we look at them with a bit of jealousy and a bit of pride.

We're crossing the border tomorrow. Most of these soldiers won't go into Iraq for their whole deployment. They eat their meals, laughing and joking. We look at them the way a pack of wolves must look at domesticated dogs.

Like we'll be fighting to survive tomorrow while these

guys will be sitting in these same seats. Like we'll be lucky to eat tomorrow while these guys just wait for a dinner call, for a pile of food in their bowls.

That night the temperature drops 30 or 40 degrees. The chill is so fast it seems to drop down my spine. This sudden chill, it's like the Grim Reaper tracing your spine with his fingernail.

I lie in the back of the dump truck trying to fall asleep, and the cold desert night even reaches me in my sleeping bag. These sleeping bags work for, like, forty below. I tell myself it's the metal of the dump truck bed. Metal's a conductor, and it sucks the cold right out of the air. I tell myself it's keeping me from falling asleep.

I climb out of the back of the 20-ton and gaze up at the mere sliver of crescent moon. I think of the old adage of God's thumbnail. In this part of the world, during this time of the year, God's thumbnail points straight down. And since the Middle East is the supposed birthplace of civilization (and Jesus and Mohammed), well, I guess that makes sense.

I take my bundled-up sleeping bag to Folden's tractor trailer. The 916 trailers have two-by-eights running down the center. These pieces of wood, unlike the metal dump bed, are insulators. They're resistant to temperature change. There are already more than a dozen soldiers claiming Folden's trailer as their bed, man-sized cocoons huddling to the center of a flatbed.

I find an empty spot and bunk down. As I fall asleep, I watch the stars. The sky here is so clear that I see five shooting stars before I doze off. That's five wishes. And they all involve tomorrow.

As we awake, we brush the frost off our sleeping bags. We pack our stuff, brush our teeth, and pee behind the vehicles' wheels. We PMCS, I open an MRE and take out the instant coffee.

MREs are the vacuum-packed meals the army gives soldiers in the field. At room temperature MREs have a shelf life of over ten years. And each little pouch of food can withstand a static load of two hundred pounds for three minutes. This means that a two-hundred-pound man could stand on top of a bag of applesauce without it bursting. The downside of this strength and stamina is everything in them tastes like salty cardboard.

I pour the powdered coffee into a Baggie and add cold water from my canteen. I use as little water as possible. That way I'm not forced to sip the coffee. Instead I take it like a shot of caffeine.

One of the maintenance guys pulls out a stick of chalk. It's good chalk that doesn't wash off easy. The maintenance platoon uses it to write on equipment, to mark it for whatever kind of maintenance reason. We use it for decoration.

One guy draws a target on his 20-ton with the exclamation "You won't do it!" Someone else writes "Iraq or Bust" on his Humvee. The 20-ton ahead of me says "C-Ya in Hell" on its rear bumper. The Lord's prayer is written on an armored 916 door. Someone else writes "Acme" on a gun turret. Another draws flames.

The rumble of thirty or so diesel engines starting wakes up the sun. It comes up as we roll out the gate of the camp. It's December 23. I joined the army exactly two years ago.

We're in Iraq. Iraq is on TV—the evening news. Being in Iraq is like being on a new planet. It's something other people do, like curing world hunger. It's something that's not supposed to happen in real life. Not to me. It's getting AIDS. It's being broken down. It's the first day of Red Phase.

A small number of the company already flew into Iraq to coordinate things for our arrival. I get to drive into Iraq. I am jealous of the advanced party. They got the easy way out: a stress-free C130 aircraft. I get a 20-ton dump truck. But all of us who have to convoy, maybe we're the lucky ones. We claim injustice, we ask why we can't all fly, but really we don't care. We didn't come to Iraq to fly over Iraq. We came here to fucking own the place.

In Kuwait we don't travel with locked and loaded magazines. When we near the border, Munoz picks up his M16, loads a magazine, and slams the bolt forward. He does the same for mine. That sound of a weapon being loaded, metal crunching together, it sounds lethal. That *click-clack*, it sounds like power.

We cross the border, and we're ready for buildings exploding, for car bombs and mushroom clouds. We're ready for bloodstains and dead bodies. I can feel my heartbeat in my throat, and I'm ready to fight my way through towns and villages. Kuwait isn't where they riot in the streets and burn the American flag. Kuwait is not where they plant roadside bombs and shoot at us. That's Iraq.

We cross the border, and we're ready to kill. We're ready to die.

We cross the border, and there are children. Little girls and little boys. Their faces are dirty with desert sand and sweat. But it's not what they look like that shocks me. It's what they do.

They see our convoy. We Americans, we're occupying their country. CNN says it's wrong, and on some level, I know it's wrong. MSNBC says the people of Iraq hate us, and on some level I know they hate us. And I know that Josh Miller—an average, redheaded farm boy—will be forced to shoot these children when they start throwing rocks at us. That's the SOP (Standard Operating Procedure).

It was covered in the convoy briefing. The "hooahs" that we yelled were forced and pathetic. "Hooah" is the army phrase that lets everyone know you're all in. Think "Tonight, men, we take that hill!" and then a crowd of scruffy guys yells, "Hooah!" from their guts. By definition hooah means anything but no. But in the briefing before we left when LT reminded us of our SOP, gave us orders to shoot children if they threw rocks, the hooahs sounded desperate, like boys acting tough.

Rocks are life-threatening when you're traveling sixty miles an hour.

Suck it up. You're a soldier and this is war.

I'm an American, and I know these children and their parents don't want me here. I know they hate me and burn my flag and drag soldiers' bodies through the streets.

Fuck 'em. I didn't choose to come here. I'm here on orders.

They want to throw rocks, I'll give them a brain full of 5.56 rounds. Put my M16 on burst. Three rounds in rapid succession. The military took the automatic option out of M16s after so much ammo was wasted in Vietnam, but they'll never take away that three-round burst. Aim low. Maybe I'll get 'em in the stomach and they'll suffer some before they bleed out. Right there on the side of the road. Right there in front of their stupid sheep.

Suck it up. This is war we're talking about, GI. This is your life we're talking about, GI Joe Schmo.

I have four men standing in the back of my dump truck. One has a mounted M60 machine gun. Another has a SAW (Squad Automatic Weapon) machine gun. The other two have M16s and hand grenades. Let's see some blood, gunners.

Throw rocks at you? You're going to let *haji* rocks take you out of the game on your first convoy? You're going to let *haji* rocks keep you from your family? That won't happen on *my* truck. Let's bathe the streets in blood, comrades.

Dozens of children line the road. They raise their hands. Their hands are empty. The kids look at Munoz and me with dark round eyes and pull their hands to their mouths. Their sheep stand in huddled masses behind them, and the children motion their empty hands to their mouths over and over again. They are begging for food.

Cold lightning drops down my spine. Tears leak into the corners of my eyes.

This is Neil Munoz's first time in Iraq, and he waves to the kids.

"Jesus," he says. "See that?"

You don't know what sadness looks like until you've seen children begging for food. Munoz rummages behind his seat, finds an open box of MREs. He tosses a few out of his window, and the kids rush to pick them up. In the side mirrors I can see the children devouring the salty, card-board meals.

This is the moment of my epiphany. When adults say, "Someday, you'll understand," this is what they're talking about. When your parents yelled at you for not finishing dinner—"There are children starving in Africa." This is why the drill sergeants told me I was stupid to be a hero. This is why we invaded Iraq.

On the side of the road: Their faces are worn. Their bodies are scrawny. Their clothes are rags. To get around, they use their feet—dirty, farmland feet that have grown up walking on rocks, thick-skinned feet that have never worn designer shoes.

The children look as if they should be in elementary school, but their eyes show wisdom I never would have understood in elementary school. These kids have wisdom I'm only beginning to grasp now. They are dirty and sweaty from working in the fields all day. They don't work to make money. They don't get allowance. They don't have part-time jobs after school busing tables so they can buy their first cars or new clothes or TV/DVD player combos for their bedrooms. They work to live. They farm crops and livestock so their family can eat.

How many kids in America can say their day-to-day efforts are a result of the struggle to survive?

Conscious of the fact that the military sees them as more of a threat than their children, the parents stand farther away from the road. They wave or hold their thumbs up, but they don't beg. In Middle Eastern culture giving is more valued than receiving. On their faces

I see them watching our convoy intently, curious as to whether or not we will throw food. Because they are hungry too.

They are not burning flags in large chaotic riots like I expected, like the evening news said. Their thumbs are up.

After six hours of driving we arrive at Camp Scania in southern Iraq for a fuel-up.

Moore is the first one to break the silence as we stand beside our long line of staged vehicles, some of us smoking cigarettes, some of us pissing behind wheel wells.

"You see those kids?" Scott Moore says.

"Yeah," we say.

"Didn't expect that," I say.

"Me neither."

There's no point in being tough about this war, this vile stomach of a country. Being tough, being bloodthirsty, no longer seems important.

Moore adds, "It breaks your heart."

After fueling we drive, past Baghdad and over the Tigris River. We pass Balad and arrive at Camp Anaconda. According to the rumors, it's not such a bad spot to end up. It's an old air base that was built in the 1980s. This means that our housing should be pretty decent. The base has been established for a while, so the chances of occupying a hard building (i.e., not a tent) are pretty good. The air force is based here, and the air force treats its servicemen about a thousand times better than the army does. They wouldn't be stationed anywhere without access to showers, and at the very least, housing trailers.

We unload our gear into our temporary homes. They call it Tent City, and it's similar to how we stayed in Kuwait. A bunch of tents dress, right, dressed as if standing in formation.

It's almost 2300 hours (eleven P.M.), and as we park the vehicles and unload our personal gear, Christmas is just around the corner. I'm standing in my tent when the clock strikes 0000.

"Merry Christmas," I say in the driest voice possible. Imagine if Christmas was a doctor's appointment. That's how much we feel like celebrating.

After a couple hours of unloading and a short briefing by the commander we bunk down. A dozen or so fold-out army cots are squished into this tent on concrete floors. On the outside rocks cover the ground. The rocks cover the dirt. Because the dirt turns to mud when it rains. And in Iraq, during winter, it rains a lot.

When we wake up in the morning, we rally between the four tents that EQ platoon occupies. LT Zeltwanger, platoon leader, stands in the middle.

"Great job on the convoy," he says. "You guys are released

for the day. Go contact your families. Tell them you love them."

He gives us information about where the phone centers are, the internet cafés, the chow hall, and the shower trailers, and gives us our mailing address so our families can send packages.

"Oh," he says. "And Merry Christmas."

I think of Heather and my parents. Back home, eight hours behind, it's about midnight. I can't call them yet, this afternoon maybe. For the last three days we've been convoying. We haven't been able to call or e-mail. Just like when we left for Kuwait, I didn't discuss specifics when I talked to them.

I know I'm safe, but I think of Heather and my parents and how hard it must be for them not to have that peace of mind. For the last few days they've been worrying, knowing that I'm driving into a war zone.

I think of past wars. Soldiers who didn't have phone access. Soldiers who didn't even know something like the Internet could even exist. I can't imagine how their families got by. Back home they'd wait weeks, months maybe, before they received word. And sometimes that word was a notification of death.

But luckily, I'll be able to call and e-mail today. Luckily, I'll be able to tell them I'm okay.

An alarm. A slow, loud alarm like a town fire alarm

back home. It echoes across the huge air base. Everyone in my tent stops and looks at one another.

"What the hell is that?" asks SGT Tim Folden.

SSG (Staff Sergeant) Lee says, "I think that's the mortar alarm."

A mortar is a flying bomb. It's manually shot into the air from a tube.

"I didn't hear anything explode," I say. But this camp is huge. It could have hit miles away or not even landed on post. It could have been a near miss. Or maybe it's a drill.

We throw on our body armor and Kevlar helmets. We don't need our weapons to fight or anything. But in the military you never, ever leave a weapon unattended. So we grab them, too, and run out of the tent. There's a nearby mortar bunker that we duck into. It's a four-foot-high tunnel of concrete shaped like a box. The openings of the tunnel are protected by stacks of sandbags.

"I think we're supposed to wait twenty minutes," says Folden.

So we wait, sitting on rocks under a box of concrete. All twelve soldiers from my tent wearing body armor and clutching M16s. Waiting to hear something explode, we GI Joe Schmos realize our war has begun.

////// THE EIGHT-HOUR DELAY //////

"We can do this one of two ways," LT Zeltwanger says to his driver, SPC Greene.

"Okay, sir," says Greene.

"There's the right way, and there's the fast way."

The lieutenant and his driver, a specialist like myself, sit in a cheaply armored Humvee. Its motor snores in neutral, staring at a large field of dirt, waiting for its driver to make a decision. This large field of dirt is to become EQ platoon's first mission.

Clearing is when a room, a service route, or a field of dirt, for example, is swept thoroughly for mines, forgotten artillery, the presence of evil doers. It's a very crucial and lifesaving step. This hasn't happened at all.

It's January 2005, and Iraq is a combat zone. In the middle of this combat zone, in an open dirt field, an entire platoon will be working, sleeping, eating, and digging shit holes for the next two weeks.

When LT asks the battalion staff whether the field has been cleared of explosives, they have no idea what he's talking about.

LT sits in the *haji* armored Humvee with twenty-year-old Greene—both of them looking at this field of dirt, hoping it won't be the last thing they ever see. They have to clear this field. The right way or the fast way.

The right way: Hands and knees. A minesweeper maybe. One cubic meter at a time. Double-check.

The fast way: No hesitation. Zigzag through the site. Turn around. Pray. Zigzag back the other way.

The entire platoon is stretched out along the road behind LT's Humvee. We're in immediate danger of attack from car bombs or mounted insurgents. We need to pull our vehicles into the field and set up a defensive perimeter.

Greene smiles at Zeltwanger.

"Better go fast," says LT. And Greene stomps the pedal to the floor.

They make their first set of connected Zs. Right away it's obvious how slow Humvees actually move when the gas is punched from a dead stop. And zigzagging through winter mud doesn't make them any faster. If something explodes, they're both so toasted. They're growing to love the adrenaline.

They zigzag back, turning their Zs into hourglasses, tied shoelaces. The field is cleared as best as it can be, and the rest of the platoon—army green 20-ton dump trucks and M916 tractor trailers carrying scoop loaders and bull-dozers—pull in.

In January in Iraq the air is chilly and the wind won't stop. Our hands are chapped and red from it. It's 70 degrees during the day and 30 at night. This 40 degree difference between day and night, it's like being on another planet.

In January it rains all the time. And the dust that covers this country doesn't mix with water. Imagine walking in a twelve-inch blanket of chunky peanut butter. Every step sinks deeper, gets heavier. It cakes up around the sides of your boots, so you have to stop and wipe it off with your chapped hands. It doesn't shake off like normal mud. Imagine boots, gear, and vehicles buried in this stuff.

Your family is eight hours away. The family you're sure won't even recognize you when you get home. The eight-hour delay between Iraq and the United States is a lifetime away.

Now you have a new family. The only family who understands you are the fifty soldiers you've grown to love.

At first you just put up with their snoring, their smell. Then you get to like them, their knack for biting sarcasm. Before you know it, you're one of them. It's like being on a wrestling team, only you're more pissed off and carrying munitions. That's a platoon of American soldiers in Iraq.

We unload the vehicles. An M16 for each of us. Some of us have SAWs. Or we have an M60, a machine gun like the SAW but with fatter bullets.

Each of us shoulders a rucksack. These portable homes, efficiently packed without an inch of wasted space, contain everything we'll need for Lord knows how long. A day? A month? Pack everything. Pack like you're not coming back.

Inside our rucksacks there are at least eight pairs of green socks and eight carbon copy brown T-shirts. There's the wet weather gear, the poncho, and the roll of 550 cord. Utility equipment to make everything from dry shelter to cover from the enemy to shade in the sun. And of course, there are the two essentials: baby wipes and deodorant. Field showers.

In our rucksacks we have the other necessities, like beef jerky, trail mix, and hand sanitizer. A deck of cards, a good book, and a flashlight with a red lens cap. The red light so *haji* can't see us.

Hanging off our rucksacks there's the sleeping bag that smells like camping, that old, dusty smell that gets all over everything. There's the E-tool (entrenching tool): a small black, collapsible shovel. We'll be using it to create extra-portable toilets. Field expedient.

Everyone unloads, fit with body armor and watchful eyes. Palm trees, orchards, and plenty of peanut butter mud for scenery. It's nine o'clock in the morning and still chilly. Our words puff clouds of steam as we talk and drink coffee. We wear polypropylene undershirts, gunner's gloves, fleece caps underneath our Kevlar helmets to keep warm.

We execute LT's plan. We unroll concertina wire and fix it to the ground. We establish fighting positions and lookout points all along our perimeter. We post guards, and they watch their "sectors of fire." All the vehicles sit in the center of our newly established "camp," all our gear scattered around them. The army look.

An hour or so later, after everything is set up, LT rallies a briefing. We stand around him in a circle. We're anxious, excited, and curious about our first mission.

LT gives a detailed briefing:

The military bridge that runs across the Tigris River, only half a mile from this point, has an entrance that isn't wide enough. The army's HEMTTs are too big to negotiate the last turn onto the bridge. The trucks keep taking out the concrete barriers that border the road there. Civilian vehicles have been hit because there is a civilian bridge that runs parallel to ours. It's a bad situation: slow moving and full of distractions.

LT explains the second part of the mission, the army's deal with the local sheik. There's a local family: mother, father, kids. They're sustenance farmers who had a bad year due to erosion. New, freshly turned soil would be a great help to them and the local economy. In exchange for our efforts, the sheik has given us this large dirt field from which we can pull land.

LT mentions our SOP about giving out food and water to civilians. He does this with a wink, because our SOP for giving out water and food is "under no circumstances," and he knows that none of us will listen.

This is not because the army doesn't care about the civilians here. It's just that there have been a few instances where kids have been run over trying to fetch a box of water or MREs from the road.

Before we leave on a convoy mission, SGT Buckelew stands as the gunner on LT's two-door Humvee. There's no armor on this vehicle, nothing to protect Buckelew from *haji*'s bombs and bullets except for dust and sunlight. He leans down and tells LT that this particular army policy is complete bullshit.

"This is a desert culture, sir," he says. "How can we accomplish anything here if we can't even share water?"

LT nods and tells Buck to make sure the last cases of water in the Humvee are strapped down. The LT would just hate to have a couple of them "accidentally" fall from the vehicle as they pulled out . . .

SSG Charles Selby is a driver and a gunner. He's a gruff and otherwise unforgiving dude. He always volunteers for the lead vehicle, probably the most dangerous spot to be in a convoy, and never hesitates under fire. He personally trained all of the heavy weapons operators and machine gunners in the company. Selby is an expert at warfare and violence. Today, he rests his arm on a case of Girl Scout cookies he just received in the mail. And he has no intentions of eating them.

LT has also been in contact with the local Iraqi police chief. He controls this part of town and wants to know what we're doing. The police chief nods at LT's explanation. The men shake hands, and the police chief asks for a favor.

Lay it on me, says LT.

Radical extremists come in the cover of night to kidnap and kill local civilians in their homes. The town is too pro-American, and civilians suffer the consequences. On random nights, the extremists' drive their Mercedes down a side road to get to the town. Conveniently enough, it runs right through our newly established camp.

"We'll take care of that right now," LT says, turning to Renninger, my squad leader. "Won't we?"

"Yes, sir," Renny replies with a satisfied grin.

Renny tosses his Marb red on the ground and jumps on a bulldozer. In all of five minutes he's built a dirt berm the size of a tank. It's a wall right across the side road with our M60 machine gun fighting position sitting right on top. No radicals will be using this road to kidnap or kill civilians anytime soon.

Later that night, sure enough, a black Mercedes, barrels down the side road. It flies by palm trees and bounces along the rough dirt road.

SGT O'Brien is on the M60, his trigger finger ready for anything.

LT Zeltwanger is next to him. "Watch this," he says.

The car's brakes lock up. Tight. They skid to a stop only feet away from the berm. It's eight o'clock, and the sun is almost down. But there's still enough light for the radicals to see the silhouettes of O'Brien and LT on the hill and the machine gun poised between them. Both LT and O'Brien are praying. *Just give us a reason to light you up, you cowardly shits.*

But they don't. The car slams into reverse, and the radicals who kill families while they're sleeping never return.

The next day, the villagers, the ones we're really fighting for, celebrate because no one was murdered the previous night. And the women of the village prepare fresh flat bread in a brick oven and bring it down to us.

For the next two weeks, with the help of B Company,

we move over 15,000 cubic yards of dirt to the bridge and the local family. We live out of our rucksacks. Baby wipe and deodorant showers. Security perimeter shifts at all times of the night. Eating MREs twice a day and digging holes for toilets.

We widen the road for the military. We cultivate dirt for the local economy. Same mission. Two different goals. Both of them equally our duty.

There's an eight-hour delay between Iraq and the United States. Millions of content American families will be sitting down for dinner eight hours from now. They'll be tired from work. Their boss doesn't give them the recognition they deserve. They'll be hungry for dinner and for the evening news. They'll be ready for the daily body count, the daily Bush-bashing, the story from Iraq. And that's all it will be to them: a story, a dramatic saga full of twists and turns and epic heroism. It'll be entertainment, the only thing they'll ever learn about the Iraq war.

They won't see this piece of war footage:

"On a mission to restore a bridge for the military and to cultivate farmland for a local Iraqi family . . ." A voice-over won't introduce . . .

SPC Jeremiah Ingold on his first mission, standing next to a Humvee. Dressed in desert camo, body armor, and a helmet, waiting for his turn on the dump truck. To his right, palm trees overlook an embankment that runs down to the Tigris River. Behind him dump trucks pour dirt into piles, bulldozers even the piles out.

Ingold watches for potential hazards. He's holding his M16, barrel down, by its pistol grip, taking a drag off the cigarette between his fingers.

And America won't see the changeover between cameras . . .

To a young Iraqi boy, no more than eight, walking down a lonely desert road toward this GI and his cigarette. This young boy wears a dirt red shirt with holes in the collar and under the armpits. He is shoeless. He is carrying a clear, plastic bottle. Its contents are speckled and brown, like water from a mud puddle. Actually, it's from the Tigris River.

The boy smiles. He waves to Ingold.

Ingold waves back. To the boy he says, "I hope you're washing your feet with that."

The boy doesn't understand.

Ingold asks him, "Are you drinking that?" and motions to his mouth with his hand.

The little boy nods.

"Oh, hell no," Ingold says to this eight-year-old without shoes.

Ingold reaches into a cardboard box in a nearby Humvee.

Content American families everywhere won't see the beaming gratitude on the boy's face when Ingold shows him what drinking water is supposed to look like: clear and sparkling. There won't be a voice-over with some cutesy little pun about a clear future for Iraq.

Because it doesn't matter either way, does it? Bombs still go off and people still die for no good reason. Good deeds mean nothing when they're cast in the shadows of bad ones, right?

America will never sit down and feel a lick of guilt as they watch this boy and this soldier in their one true moment of glory. Because, unlike this little boy who won't be on their televisions, they've never had tears in their eyes over a bottle of water.

They'll never see . . .

The way our efforts are shunned. At first we don't care. In a way it makes us proud. It's humility. And selfless service is truly selfless if you're never recognized. *All in due time*, we tell ourselves. *America will know. All in due time.*

This is what we say. This is what we actually believe. The truth always comes out in the end. But somehow the truth doesn't come out.

So there's nobility. Hanging on for the sake of sharing our story. Because we realize that the truth can come only through us. So we tell people. We yell it right in their ears. But these letters and e-mails, they never break out further than with our family members. For the bad news is what people want to hear. Oh, sure, it's still the truth. The half of the truth that sells newspapers.

And this truth is what buries us in frustration. We become consumed with anger. No acceptance, no sympathy. Just pure, boiling anger. The way people don't understand, the way they can't understand—it's like a back alley full of hot metal. The only people who understand are stuck here with us, feeling the same outrage and same fear that we'll die without a chance to share our story.

And there's nothing we can do. No words or e-mails or made-for-TV movies we can produce to show our side. No Iraq war memoir that can explain what it feels like to watch our efforts kicked out of the way for the juicy car bomb footage. The good things we do and did, and the way our country tries to take those away from us.

"Support the Troops" isn't the way people feel. It's a slogan. Just like "The War on Terror." Just like "We Will Never Forget."

Anger is lonely.

It's the sheer loneliness of manning a .50 caliber machine gun at two o'clock in the morning. It's a cold, wet perimeter watch on our first mission. It's gazing up at the empty desert sky.

In the center of a Middle Eastern desert, no moon out, our platoon running in blackout, and the night sky. The Milky Way, no longer just milky but a streak of white paint. It's opaque and filled with brilliance that can't be seen through the polluted mess we call air in the United States.

I slip on the night vision goggles. You have no idea how many stars there are. I once heard that for every grain of sand on the earth, there is a star in the sky. I never believed it until I saw the sky in night vision. At least three shooting stars per minute. All night long.

There's so much beauty and no one with which to share it. I am alone.

No one really wants to hear this story. And no one who hears this story will truly hear it. For the beauty of war is surrounded by the gruesome. And that damn eight-hour delay filtering everything.

///////////// THE TOWN THAT ///////////// ACHMED BUILT

We move out of Tent City and into a concrete building. The best thing about a hard building is no more mortar bunkers, just report inside. But there is some work to be done if we want to live comfortably.

The best part about being engineers is our access to supplies. Most units would have to find another unit, probably engineers, that would be willing to give them supplies. The paperwork could take weeks. Longer if it wasn't for something necessary, like comfortable quarters.

So when we move into our new barracks, we have plywood and 2x4s, hammers and nails, power drills, and rotary saws. And we have MOSs that say we know how to build stuff.

There's a large bay in the barracks filled with bunk beds and wall lockers, sort of like we had in Fort Bragg. But this isn't Bragg. We have to live here for a year. And that means we want our privacy. We build ourselves some partitions. Think plywood cubicles.

Sergeant Folden and Sergeant Lee, the two head sergeants in first squad, run the show. Like a classic duo, Tim Folden is tall and thin and Jeremy Lee is short and stocky. Just like Jay and Silent Bob in *Clerks*.

I am given a room in one of the "lower enlisted" bays for privates and specialists.

The leadership bay is for the sergeants of the platoon. The plywood walls in this bay form the main hallway as you come into the barracks. The leadership rooms are bigger than the lower enlisted rooms, second only to the rooms of the squad leaders, platoon leader, and platoon sergeant.

After a week of building the whole platoon settles down in its new plywood rooms. Plywood doesn't sound very luxurious, but at least we have some privacy, a place we can call home. In Fort Bragg we slept in an open bay. In Camp Virginia it was a tent with cots. On the convoy it was the trailer of an M916. And until recently at Anaconda it was a tent with cots. Finally, we're in a hard building with actual metal-framed beds and walls separating us from one another.

I lie in my bunk for the first night thinking of accomplishing my first mission and wonder what is supposed to happen next.

My purpose, I conclude, is to understand the point of this deployment. To understand why the drill sergeants said, "There's no such thing as an atheist in a foxhole."

On EQ platoon's next mission, we watch war happen. What's different about the Iraq war from any other is that there aren't "front lines." But we come pretty close on our second mission.

Loud. Decrepit. Nauseating. Decayed. Heavily populated.

A place I will never forget. It overflows with destruction, oozes the rotten stench of death, and hatred.

This is Samarra, Iraq.

This is the town that Achmed built.

We are not soldiers to our commander; we are bodies. "I need four bodies to send on the convoy tomorrow," he says. "Give me two bodies to help carry these supplies for the motor sergeant."

"Pack your gear," he yelled at the mission briefing a week ago. "Clean your weapons, and send a letter home to your family."

We write every letter as if it's our last. In my letters I tell my family I love them. Little else matters.

"When you contact your loved ones," he tells us, "do not disclose information that may be threatening to the mission. I say again . . ." He repeats himself two more times. OPSEC.

He knows that if the wrong person overhears us and our mission is foiled, he'll have to do the mess of bureaucratic planning again. We know that if the wrong person overhears us and our mission is foiled, it could mean our lives.

We're leaving on a new mission. A dangerous mission. An exciting mission. One that could look great on the commander's credentials. One that requires almost all of our platoon. Almost all of our bodies.

We don't care. We live for this. We are carved out of stone, ready to handle anything. LT Andy Zeltwanger, he knows how to motivate us, how to mold us. Our lieutenant bands us together like cement binds rock.

We have to stick together. For survival.

We enter the city today as we've done it a hundred times before. Iraqi Army soldiers patrol the streets like the way the police covered sixties' civil rights protests. Every day soldiers are scattered about the city at various checkpoints, but today they are everywhere. They wave to us and continue to patrol. The city depends on them for protection.

It's Thursday. The insurgents with a jihad on their agendas want to kill infidels today and brag to God tomorrow.

Tomorrow is Friday, the Muslim holy day. By the way, an infidel is not Christian. An infidel is not Jewish or Buddhist or Hindu. An infidel is not an American or a Brit or an Australian. An infidel is anyone who doesn't support the murder of infidels. What a convenient, self-serving philosophy.

Infidels can be, and often are, Muslim. The same Muslims who sit at the local mosque and pray for peace. This town is full of them.

These are the people that live in the town that Achmed built.

An orange bubble rises from the ground. It is a hundred yards away and growing bigger, higher, brighter. The sound catches up to it. A popping roar like a thousand synchronized fireworks. I feel the percussion blast in my head, in my chest, in my legs.

The bottom of the orange bubble caves in on itself as the explosion turns into a black mushroom cloud. I see body parts flying through the air.

Dismembered people. ·

I know the location where that bomb exploded. It's smack in the middle of our route out of the city. We've driven through it many times before. We were on our way there. It's a populated area full of markets and homes. I have a sickening hunch that those body parts belong to women and children. Infidels.

This is the bomb that killed the people . . .

We are stuck in the middle of this armpit of a city. The metallic smell of gunpowder and the dusty smell of broken concrete fill my nose. We are stuck, and people are dying. People have died.

I want to scream. I want to cry. I want to run.

Instead, I am watching death rain pieces of children from the sky. They will not wake up tomorrow. They are infidel hamburger.

I sit in this sorry excuse for a dump truck as the machine-gun fire starts.

These are the guns that accompany the bomb . . .

In the middle of downtown Samarra a small American infantry base sits in a square block of rubble. Buildings surround the rubble on all sides. Fifty yards lie between the base and the nearest street. The infantry tanks have to use this route when they go on missions. Problem is, insurgents come in the cover of night and bury mines outside their main gate. So far, they've lost three tanks.

"We'll take care of it," we tell them. "We'll bring gravel in trucks and dump it outside your base. Shovels can't dig through rocks."

For a week we've been running small rocks from a pit. One way, the ride is two hours. We make two runs per day. Sometimes things hold us up and we make only one run. Today the insurgents hold us up.

These are the insurgents that fire the guns . . .

We had a long day yesterday, too. We're running on two hours of sleep, and we haven't eaten anything except MREs. We are tired and hungry, but it doesn't matter. We do not care about our rumbling stomachs or heavy eyelids.

The explosion, it's like the first snowball of an avalanche. It sets off reactions in my body I didn't know existed. The adrenaline pumping through my veins could power a city. It could melt steel. Stop bullets.

People are screaming and dying and burning and dying.

This is the death that drives the insurgents . . .

I watch my "sector of fire." My training kicks in. I do not make panicked decisions. Rubble from previous battles is laid out before me. Unidentifiable pieces of broken concrete and messy rebar blend together on the ground. I pay no attention to the people dying to my left. I watch my sector: a 90-degree angle fanning outward across the broken, spiritless city. If everyone watches his sector, we make a 360-degree perimeter of overlapping fire.

Impenetrable.

Thirty yards away, in my sector of fire, I watch the house we took fire from the other day. We could not get to the triggerman. He was a coward taking cheap shots at us. If LT hadn't turned at the right moment, he would have been shot in the chest. When we took fire, four tanks rolled out and blew Triggerman away. I couldn't tell if they killed him, but we haven't taken fire from that house since.

I watch that house like a hawk.

But the tanks can't help us out right now. Our convoy is hanging out of their small base. We block their route. We are blocking our own route to get back in. Whatever wreckage caused by the bomb is probably blocking our path ahead. We dare not take our chances on the narrow road.

This is the road that harbors the death . . .

I am stuck "outside the wire" in the passenger seat of a 20-ton dump truck, and my weapon, an M16, hangs out of my window. Its selector switch is no longer on safe. I click it to semi. I click it again. That's burst.

Every squeeze of the trigger equals three bullets. Fast, three rounds in succession. LT made sure we loaded our magazines so that every fourth bullet is a tracer. Think of those yellow streaks you see in Vietnam movies. If things are moving too fast to use the sights, we aim off the tracers.

Aim low. With a three-round burst your rifle will unavoidably kick upward along the front of the target. Aim low and you're bound to hit him once. If you're lucky, you'll land two. Land all three and you're Green Beret material.

We wait for direction. I watch my sector.

We sit on top of a foot and a half of gravel we've poured over the last week, and we are under our own firepower: Humvees are mounted with .50 caliber machine guns and

M60 machine guns and ammo box after ammo box, and AT4 rocket launchers hang off their turrets. On our person we have fragment grenades and smoke grenades and M16 semiautomatic rifles and M203 grenade launchers and SAWs. LT takes no chances when it comes to firepower. Not here. Not in the town that Achmed built.

I wait. Nothing in my sector.

A stray bullet whizzes by from somewhere. A high-pitched whistle. It has missed any target it was intended for. I duck into my body armor like I could actually dodge a screaming bullet. It's a reflexive maneuver meant to keep me alive. Because I know our trucks are cheaply armored. Half-ass, *haji* armor on the door. It's better than nothing. Maybe. Just more shrapnel.

Another bullet whistles by. I duck.

A metallic slap. A bullet bounces off the dump ahead of me.

These are the bullets that fly from the road . . .

Finally, some direction. The fighting has hit a crucial point: the eye of the storm. LT has a chance to initiate a plan. Over the radio he tells the gun trucks to exit the convoy.

"Create a perimeter," he commands, "and give the dumps room to turn around. Over."

Three or four gun trucks pull out. One parks directly in front of me. I raise my rifle so I don't accidentally send three bullets into the M60 gunner who's taken over my sector. The 20-ton ahead of us moves, and my driver pulls a tentative foot off the brake.

The rapid gunfire continues.

"Stay behind the gunners," the lieutenant reminds the dump trucks.

The turreted Humvees sit on broken rubble from previous battles. They can drive over anything. They sit like a militant version of Stonehenge.

In the Humvees the driver waits with watchful eyes. The radio man sits in the passenger seat and relays radio messages to the rest of his crew. His hand is two inches away from the gunner's foot. He is ready to rattle the gunner's leg and mark targets with a time designation. Twelve o'clock is straight ahead. Six o'clock is right behind. Three to the right, and nine to the left.

An ammo guy sits behind the driver with an eager hand resting on box upon box of ammunition. He's got one open. His palms are sweaty and he absentmindedly thumbs the next round that has to be handed up to the gunner. Hot, expended rounds are dropping through the hole in the roof where the gunner stands. They are smoking and bouncing and clinking.

The gunner is the backbone of the gun truck. His posture against the weapon's kickback is stiff and unforgiving. His Kevlar helmet rattles with the ricochet of the .50 cal.

His dark gunner goggles bounce beneath them. His body armor is strategically loaded with fragment grenades and smoke grenades, ammo pouches and a bayonet, a medical pouch and a pair of utility pliers. Each piece is stuck to him like paint to a hard canvas. It's 90 degrees out, but the gunner wears gloves. The black metal weapon absorbs the desert heat. If he doesn't wear gloves, he'll get blisters from holding the trigger down.

A Humvee crew is a team. Think of limestone and clay. Think of adding calcium sulfate and water. That's how you bind rocks.

We move inside the gate, and the gun trucks stay behind. A half dozen tanks wait for the congestion to thin out. The last dump finds its way, and the tanks roll, throwing dust in circular clouds behind them. They split and wage war in the city streets.

These are the tanks that avenge the bullets . . .

The gun trucks have accomplished their mission. They return to the safety of the base. We hear explosions for another hour as the tanks avenge the ambush on the engineer convoy.

Military Intelligence would later inform the LT that the ambush didn't go quite as planned. The untrained insurgent set off the explosion prematurely. He killed himself. His untrained insurgent allies were all lined up and down the street ready for holy victory. The triggerman was supposed to throw the switch on our first vehicle, thus trapping our cumbersome dump trucks on the narrow road. Instead, he spoiled the plan with a sweaty trigger finger, taking out four Iraqi Army soldiers and seven civilians with him.

No Americans. All infidels.

I think of the consequences if the plan had been carried out with success. We would have been stuck in the middle of downtown Samarra with crappy do-it-yourself armor. Insurgents would have been feet away from our vehicles sinking round after round into our weak armor. Gun trucks would pull out, but they would have no leverage. Not compared to men on their feet. A gunner can't aim straight down in front of him. The ambush would have taken out many more infidels.

This is the ambush that deploys the tanks . . .

My driver and I, our adrenaline rushes slowing down, listen intently as the fifteen vehicles in the convoy call in their ACE reports to the LT. An ACE (Ammo, Casualties, Equipment) report is a quick and easy way to estimate the standing of an entire convoy. Green means full or good; yellow means some or slight; red means none or very, very bad. An ideal ACE report is your call sign and green, green, green.

"Hunter Six, this is Hunter One. Yellow, green, green. Over."

"Roger. Out," LT responds calmly. If he's calm, we're calm.

"Hunter Two. Green, green, green. Over."

"Roger, Two. Out."

There's slight apprehension while we wait for the reports to come in. If anyone had taken a casualty, we'd probably know about it by now. Still, we hardly breathe.

The ACE reports are done. No casualties. How did that happen? It doesn't matter. We are alive.

We are the soldiers who survive the ambush that deployed the tanks that avenged the bullets that flew from the road that harbored the death that drove the insurgents that fired the guns that accompanied the bomb that killed the people that live in the town that Achmed built.

So many questions follow the ambush in Samarra. What was the purpose for the loss of life? Was the loss of the eleven Iraqis *my* gain? Does *my* life hold a higher value? Do I pity their calamity or honor their sacrifice? Am I lucky to have survived or unlucky to have witnessed those who didn't? Does my life become troubled with guilt or more meaningful? What makes true sacrifice worthwhile?

It is my full responsibility to give purpose to myself, to my family, and to your freedom.

For the infidels.

When we're not on missions like the one in Samarra, there is work to be done back at camp, filling sandbags or stacking sandbags, flattening patches of bumpy gravel in some parking lot on post. Or PMCSing vehicles and getting ready for upcoming missions.

Busy work, we say. Sometimes, the command calls them "missions," to motivate us, I guess. We reserve the "mission" title for something at least quasi-dangerous. We call the on-post, or "inside the wire," operations "tasks."

Most of the time our tasks are boring and tedious. Sometimes they're strenuous and demanding. Sometimes they're meaningless and irritating. They're things we've done a thousand times, like a PMCS, things we could do in our sleep.

But every once in a while a task is as interesting as a mission.

Today, like most other days, the majority of the platoon is out on various missions. Some are outside the wire convoying. And some are stuck inside the wire pushing gravel around, pulling security shifts, moving concrete barriers to make mortar cover, hauling lumber and supplies around post, loading tractor trailers. Some of the platoon is inside other wires helping the line companies, staying at their camps, pushing around their gravel, moving their lumber and supplies. Engineering stuff.

Our job, it's always different. Every day, mostly, we change gears. This is a good thing. I hear about the snipers on post. Cool job, right, being a sniper? No, it downright sucks here. Snipers sit in a guard tower all day, for thirteen months now.

Our camp gets mortared quite a bit. But the enemy is smarter than you'd think. During the hottest part of the day, they've figured out a way to fire mortars and disappear before a sniper or QRF (Quick Reaction Force) has a chance to get them.

They set up the mortar tube, aim it at camp, drop in a chunk of ice, and then drop a mortar round. When the ice melts, the round falls down the tube, gets primed, and *ka-blam!* A mortar lands somewhere on post, ruins something. And a whole camp of soldiers is squatting in mortar bunkers.

Our enemies are cowards. They take potshots at us from alleyways, drop ice in mortar tubes. They don't rush bases. They'd be killed instantly. Probably by the snipers. So every day this team of snipers, they sit in a guard tower with their binoculars reporting suspicious vehicles and people to the post command.

Not to downplay the snipers' role in this war. They save lives, and the potential for attack is high. But being a sniper probably sounded much more exciting when those guys were sitting in a MEPS station back home.

Engineers, though, we're doing pretty much what they said we'd be doing in AIT. And at least our busy work keeps us busy. It gives us something to write home about, something to keep our minds off the fact that we're stuck here.

Today a few of us mill around the barracks. It's one of our off days. There isn't much to do, even in the way of tasks. We've already done our PMCSes, cleaned the barracks. It's ten o'clock and the half dozen of us stuck without any mission or task plan on hiding out for the rest of the day.

The desert is starting to live up to its reputation. It doesn't rain anymore. In fact, I haven't seen a single cloud in weeks. And the temperature is climbing. It's only February and the days are creeping up around 90.

We hang out in the common area and play poker and dominos. We watch movies and stay out of the heat. We play the guitar and share stories and laugh. Who cares? We got back from a mission two days ago, a convoy to drop off supplies for Charlie company, and there's another mission coming up.

Who cares? The commander, the higher-ups. That's who.

"Look busy," says Renninger, grinning as he walks by, heading toward the door.

He understands our need to relax, but his words are what matter. If the guys in his squad are caught slacking around, Renninger is the one who gets yelled at.

"We are busy, Sergeant," says Josh Roman, pointing to the yellow bucket full of gray mop water.

Renninger laughs and repeats, "Look busy."

When he opens the door, blinding sunlight shines off our tile floor. He passes LT and the two stop to talk quickly.

LT comes inside, removes his patrol cap, and smiles at us. He sighs.

"Something the matter, sir?" I ask.

He shakes his head and puts up a hand. This is his way of letting me know that something is wrong, but he can't talk about it. Some nonsense with the commander, I'm sure.

"Smithson," says LT.

"Yes, sir?"

"What's the best part about being in Iraq?"

"Nothing."

"Wrong," he says. "One way or another, you know you're going to leave."

We all laugh.

"Even if they have to take me home in a pine box," he says, "I'll be the hell out of here."

"Or if they have to take you in handcuffs because you killed the commander," I say.

"I saw him walking to chow with gloves on yesterday," says Koprowski.

"He wipes the dirt off his Humvee tire before he uses it," says Roman.

"It's okay," says LT. "I use it against him. 'Neat freak' doesn't even begin to describe your commander. I think he has a coaster for his coaster."

We all laugh, not doubting for a second that he does.

"Before I went into the CQ (Command Quarters), I was out helping Greene PMCS our Humvee," says LT. "And we greased it."

We all cringe, laughing. Greasing a vehicle is one of the messiest jobs an engineer can do. Picture a tube of grease the size of a tube of raw cookie dough. It's pumped out of the end, and it always slops out on your hands. This grease, it doesn't even come off with soap. The ground just makes your hands dusty, so you wipe the grease on your uniform.

"So I sit down," LT says. "Right on his bed."

"God damn!" says Sebastian Koprowski. Seabass, we call him.

"And I can see him just . . . crawling up the wall. My greasy uniform is all over his bed, and his eyes get as wide as golf balls. And I say, 'This is a nice room, sir' as I lean on his pillow."

We're all laughing hysterically, picturing the commander squirm in his clean, pressed uniform as LT just lounges all over his bed.

"So he pulls out this little fold-out chair. And I'm like, 'No, thanks. Your bed is so comfortable, sir.'"

"He probably washed the sheets as soon as you left," I say.

"Smithson," says LT, "I'd bet my rank he burned them."

"God damn!" Seabass says again.

"Oh, man," says LT, shaking his head. "I'm going to get arrested for talking to you guys like this."

"It's not like we don't already know, sir," says Buckelew.

"Yeah, still," says LT. "Hey, Zerega, can I get you and two guys to meet Sergeant Whisler by those Humvees. You know the ones that just came in?"

"Yes, sir," says Sergeant Zerega.

Zerega grabs Roman and me, and we follow him out the front door.

Our motor pool is filled with gravel to keep down the mud, and now that the mud is drying, to keep down the dust. Dozens of vehicles are lined up, waiting for a mission or task or yet another PMCS.

Near the middle of the motor pool lie two Humvees.

"Have you seen these yet?" Zerega asks us as we approach them. Roman says yes, and I say no.

"Came in a few days ago," he says. "Guess a couple of guys died in 'em."

This doesn't really affect me. This is a war. People die.

Two blown-up Humvees side by side. They're black and charred. Our task: scrounge for parts, armor mostly. We're to take off the armor that is still intact and put it on our own Humvees. Some of which aren't armored at all.

The smell is the first thing I notice. It's an odd mixture of scorched rubber, smoldering hair, burnt metal, and . . . something else. There is an underlying stench of cooked meat. It reminds me of ham, but I know that's not what it is.

It rolls my stomach a bit, but I deal with it.

We poke around one of them for a minute or two. The thing's insides are coated with a dusty black residue. It's from the IEDs (Improvised Explosive Devices) that destroyed them.

We are curious. We poke around because this is a rare opportunity, this taste of death. Right in the charred black seat where we're poking and prodding.

That's what death does. It defines life. What would life be without death? What would death be without life? And what would peace be without war? Without the distinction nothing exists.

Really, death and war are everything.

I feel immense sorrow for those who were killed here, for their families. But at the same time, I feel immense relief knowing that there's one more KIA, one more statistic, that isn't me.

Whisler has already removed an armored door frame that he's drilled in order to modify to our own. He continues to work off to the side as Zerega, Roman, and I poke around the blackened, charbroiled Humvee.

We find a piece of desert uniform. It's about four inches by four inches and has a seam running through its middle. I hold it next to various seams of my own uniform. Maybe an elbow? But it was found next to the gas pedal. It was a knee. It's gray from the bomb residue and partially blood-stained. It smells like burnt ham.

We find several pieces of shrapnel. Thick, twisted chunks of metal. One of them has small vertical scratches running along the top. They are close together and parallel. They're from the metal band that held the IED round together. It's from a .133 or .155 round. I look at those tick marks, and it occurs to me that someone has looked at these ticks before. Someone who hates me. Someone who doesn't even know me. Someone who's killed my fellow soldiers. I feel my eyes narrow, and I throw the piece of shrapnel back into the mess of miscellaneous junk sitting in the middle of the Humvee.

We find a thin piece of metal. It's army green and shaped like a potato chip, as though it was melted, deformed, and solidified. It's a piece of an ammo can. The ammo can that held 5.56 rounds for a SAW. Some empty 5.56 shells lie nearby. They're expended, but we realize that they were not shot. The actual bullets are gone; they had been blasted into a seat or a door or a person. The casings are all that's left over, but they're mangled and ripped apart.

The IED blast was so hot and so fast that bullets were heated to a point beyond their tolerance. They cooked off. Imagine how intense an explosion would have to be to cook off rounds. Imagine what that could do to flesh.

"Look at this," says Zerega from the passenger side of the vehicle.

The passenger door is riddled with ball bearings. Hundreds of pebble-sized balls of metal packed together and exploding like buckshot. They're stuck halfway in the door and surrounding armor.

On the inside of the armor the door is wavy with

impressions, but there are no holes where the ball bearings made it through. The armor worked. On the door, anyway.

The bottom side of this Humvee wasn't armored, and the shrapnel came through the passenger floor.

The cushion on the passenger's seat is army green, but coated in the black of bomb residue and the brown of dried blood. Someone died right here. I imagine it in slow motion.

The shrapnel, hundreds of scorching ball bearings, coming through the floor ripping the passengers apart like pulled pork. Chunks of flesh and bone flying through the cabin. Their aortas bleed out over their body armor. A hot, red river of life being lost.

Enough.

"What do you want us to do first, Sergeant?" I ask Whisler.

"I need the brackets from that passenger door," he says, and goes back to drilling holes in the receiving Humvee's door frame.

I grab a socket wrench and reach into the crack between the seat and the door frame. Looking for a bolt, I see something in the dark space. It's a small square. I reach into the crack with my knife and poke it. I can't poke into it, but its peculiar texture is one which requires more examination. I pour water into the crack and the square loosens up. It's spongy, and now I can stick it with my knife.

Pulling it out of the darkness, I examine it closely. It's about the size of a quarter and roughly the same color. Like everything else in the Humvee, it's the gray-black of death.

Curly black hairs stick out of it. Actually, they've grown from it. There are circular pockets of white. It's human flesh.

I study it like I'm a biology student. Seabass usually busts my balls for picking my teeth with this knife after chow. I tell him it gets the job done as good as any toothpick. But this knife won't be picking my teeth anymore.

I fling the meat back into the hole from which it was taken. Like a burial.

I continue unscrewing the bracket for the armored door.

Zerega, Roman, Whisler, and I joke around like we always do. We make fun of the commander and make fun of each other. We unscrew, unfasten, cut, grind, drill, and transfer parts from the old Humvees to the new ones. Then it comes time to transfer the armored roofs.

It takes all four of us to lift the roof off the old Humvee and place it on the ground. We set it down and we stop, just staring at it.

The two frames, centered on either side, cause the whole roof to tip forward when we put it down. It sits on the dirty, hard ground like a wide, armored seesaw. But you wouldn't want to sit on this seesaw. One half of the roof is covered with a dusty brown bloodstain.

The SAW gunner's blood.

I imagine a young kid standing in the hole of a gun turret, loading the SAW he's loaded a hundred times. *Click-clack*, metal crunching together. But today it's not a sound of power. It sounds like fate. I see the kid just standing there, helpless as he takes a black cloud to the face. Hidden in the black cloud, hot ball bearings that end his life. Right here on this tan roof.

I imagine the kid driving the Humvee. Some kid out of high school who didn't know what he wanted to do with life. His panic as he tries to swerve away from the IED. His guilt as the warm gunner's blood drips down the back of his neck from the roof.

I should cry, I think. That's what normal people would do, right? But what does crying do for us? It doesn't solve our problems. It doesn't make us run faster or shoot better.

But it's not this logic that's keeping me from crying. I can't cry because I don't feel anything. Seeing blood, speckled brown blood, takes the feeling, the life, right out of me.

"We're gonna have to spray this off," someone finally says.

We use a small forklift and bring the bloody thing over

to the pressure washer, which lies on the other side of the motor pool. Whisler takes hold of the hose and begins spraying the dusty blood off the roof. The water carries the blood to the dirt.

Recycling, I think.

Whisler hits a pocket, maybe from the turret, and the blood-water sprays into his mouth. Whisler throws the hose to the ground and spits out dirty brown water.

I imagine that smell of burnt meat and metal. I imagine it in my mouth. And I cringe just watching Whisler spit out the dirty water.

Zerega almost keels over because he's laughing so hard.

"Oh, God," says Whisler.

"Oh, God," cries Zerega. "You ate brains! You ate brains! Oh, my God!"

"Shut up," says Whisler, wiping his tongue on his sleeve.

"Zombie!" Zerega points and laughs. "You ate brains! Zombie!"

"I think I'm going to puke," says Whisler.

But he doesn't. Zerega's laugh is maniacal. I almost admire it. Why cry when you can laugh?

Over the next week the four of us scrub, strip, and scrap the old Humvees. Part of the job is taking a putty knife to the foam that lines the inside of the roof. The foam is riddled with chunks of skull and shrapnel. It's splattered with blood and bomb residue, so we scrape it off and throw it away.

Before we put it in the Dumpster, though, we offer the pieces to Whisler. We just know he's starving for some good human brain. And we check the sergeant's eyes in the morning to see if they've glazed over and turned yellow. We watch our backs when he's around, afraid he'll try to sneak a bite out of the fleshy part of our shoulders or necks.

We joke about the death we encounter, even these little tastes. Because when it's humorous, it's not scary or sad. We can't dictate fear. We can't control sadness. These feelings are beyond our reach. But we can control sarcasm, irony.

In a lot of ways it's our humor that allows us to conquer death. It's our humor that lets us live. Even if it's temporary, just for a day, it's survival. We have to rise above death. We have to laugh in its face.

PART II
//////// WHITE PHASE ////////

nly after we have been completely destroyed can we begin to find ourselves.

The drill sergeants do it like this: they break us down, build us up, break us down again, and then build us back up. The first breakdown is the hardest part. It's the first three weeks, and they call it Red Phase.

The second three weeks, White Phase, is when they build us up.

We stand in formation outside the brick barracks on the Monday of the fourth week, completely destroyed, anticipating moving to White Phase. The red guidon waves in the Missouri wind at the front of our formation. We're so sick of that flag, that bloody red flag. We want the white one. We want to move on, to grow and learn. We want to leave the last three weeks behind us.

The drill sergeant comes out with a folded cloth in his hand. It's white. I can almost sense everyone in the platoon smiling. He takes the flagpole from the guidon bearer and, instead of changing the flag, he yells, "Front leaning rest position, move."

This means push-up position.

"Congratulations, fourth platoon," he says. "You fail again."

Then he says, "Down . . ."

"Attention to detail!" we yell.

"You think you deserve White Phase?"

No one says a word.

"In no way have you little hemorrhoids shown me you deserve this white flag," he says.

Then he says, "Up . . ."

"Work as a team!"

"You make me sick!" he yells. "You can't agree with each other. You don't help each other on the confidence courses. You hardly deserve the *red* flag.

"Down . . ." he says.

"Attention to detail!"

"Oh, and by the way," he says, "the drill sergeant on duty yesterday informed me that I have an atheist in my platoon."

Silence.

"Is that true?" he says.

"Yes, Drill Sergeant," says the atheist.

"Well, you know what they say, don't you?"

"Yes, Drill Sergeant."

"Well?"

Silence.

"I can keep you in the front leaning rest all day, Antichrist," says the drill sergeant.

"Drill Sergeant..." she starts, stammers. "Drill Sergeant, there's no such thing as an atheist in a foxhole."

"You're damn right," he says.

Then he waits, we're holding ourselves four inches off the ground. Silence and the burn of worked muscles. He walks to the front of the formation, "Up . . ."

"Work as a team!"

"Position of attention, move."

We stand back up. The drill sergeant hands the flagpole back to the guidon bearer and puts the white flag in his cargo pocket.

"I'm marching you to the arms room to draw dummy weapons," he tells us. "Today, we start BRM."

Like every other training, BRM, or Basic Rifle Marksmanship, has a crawl, walk, and run phase. Three steps—like red, white, and blue—to ensure we're experts. The crawl phase of BRM starts with dummy weapons.

Rubber rifles, sometimes called rubber duckies, that are the same size and weight as real M16s.

The first thing we do with the rubber duckies is "rifle PT." On the march back to the barracks from the arms room, we don't call cadence loud enough. We don't deserve White Phase, and our punishment is rifle PT.

Neither the M16 nor its rubber counterpart is very heavy: about eight pounds. But press either over your head two-hundred times and it's heavier than granite. Squat for ten minutes while holding a rubber ducky straight out in front of you, and just marching to chow the next day is a challenge.

The purpose of the rubber duckies is to get us used to handling M16s—which are a meter long, and not to mention, lethal. We have to know how to interact with one and the safest way to manage it. This is partly the reason for rifle PT.

"Your weapon," yells the drill sergeant, "is an extension of your body. It is a part of you. You will not leave it dirty. You will not leave it behind."

Holding a weapon lying on your stomach is called the prone position. Picture fifty privates lying in chopped-up tire pieces, propped up on one elbow, aiming their fake rubber rifles at nothing.

"Roll left," says the drill sergeant, his voice echoing off the barracks that surround us.

He means roll like a barrel. One full turn to the left, then stop. The trick is to keep your muzzle off the ground.

"Your weapon," says the drill sergeant, "is your best friend. You will take care of it. And it will take care of you.

"Roll right."

Fifty privates in the prone position roll like barrels, then stop.

"Your weapon," says the drill sergeant, "is unbiased. It does not care where you are from. Or what color your skin is. Or your religion. And don't think for a minute that your weapon cares about what's between your legs.

"Rush."

He means three to five seconds. In your head, as you jump up and run, you think, *I'm up.* . . . *He sees me.* . . . *I'm down.* That should be three to five seconds. Fifty privates jump up, run ten meters, drop down. Little chunks of tire bounce up around them. The trick is to keep your muzzle off the ground.

"Your weapon," says the drill sergeant, "does not know how to miss. It fires perfect every time. Your weapon cannot be blamed for a bad shot. Your weapon cannot be blamed for anything.

"Low crawl."

This means on your stomach, keeping your head low. The smell of rubber is so close it becomes the taste of rubber. And there's the familiar sting of lactic acid coating my shoulders as I try to keep the muzzle off the ground.

"Your weapon," says the drill sergeant, "does not kill your enemy. You kill your enemy."

After a few days of carrying, marching, and rolling around with the rubber rifles we draw real ones. In the training bay of the barracks, we lie in the prone position and practice aiming at paper targets, little silhouettes of men. We practice putting the front sight post on his torso.

The front sight post aims the barrel of the weapon. The rear aperture aims the chamber. In order to hit the target the front sight post needs to be in the center of the rear aperture. This is called the sight picture.

When we're steady enough in the prone, we put a penny on the end of the muzzle. When you pull the trigger, if the penny falls, it's ten push-ups. The trick to pulling a trigger is not pulling. It's squeezing. Concentrating on your index finger, tighten your fist. Don't pull with your arm. Pull, and the sight picture moves, the whole rifle moves. And if the rifle moves, the penny falls. That's ten push-ups. In a combat zone, that's your life.

Another thing: don't breathe. Breathe while firing and the penny falls. Patience is key. Attention to detail. Being aware of your body and its patterns. There's a natural pause at the end of an exhale. That's when you shoot. Holding your breath too long can make the rifle jittery. You have to relax.

The fifth week, while we're still waiting to go to White

Phase, morale is low and the fourth platoon training bay is silent. Five privates lie on the buffed tile floor concentrating, each holding an M16. Five lines of privates stand behind them. And five privates squat next to the ones in the prone. Each balances a penny on the end of his battle buddy's muzzle.

One at a time, *clack*: the sound of the rifle's hammer falling. The sound that would be a *bang* if there was a bullet in the chamber. But this is walk phase; there are no bullets.

And then, the one lonely *clink-clink* of a penny falling. The drill sergeant doesn't say a word. The private whose penny falls places his weapon on the tops of his hands (you never put a rifle on the ground) and knocks out ten push-ups. His battle buddy does them, too. No private should ever be punished alone. Because no soldier should ever be alone.

The privates who squeezed their triggers successfully move on. Each stands up, hands his weapon to the next private in line, and then squats to place a penny on the barrel.

The private whose penny fell lies back down and tries again, his whole line waiting for him.

Think relay race. The first line to get everyone through successfully gets to pick the exercise for the rest of the platoon. When the winner is declared, the drill sergeant tells them to discuss the punishment they want everyone else to do.

"What's it going to be?" the drill sergeant asks the winners.

"Drill sergeant," says one of the privates, "we pick flutter kicks."

"My favorite," says the drill sergeant. "Which one of you is going to call cadence?"

"Drill sergeant," says the private, "we're going to do them, too."

"Okay," says the drill sergeant. To the platoon he says, "The flutter kick."

"The flutter kick," we repeat.

"Starting position, move."

We lie on our backs and lift our feet off the ground.

"And begin," says the drill sergeant. "One, two, three . . ."

"One," we yell.

"One, two, three . . ."

"Two."

After number thirty the drill sergeant says, "Halt."

He says, "Position of attention, move."

And we stand.

At formation for dinner chow the drill sergeant walks out of the barracks with a white flag. He takes down the red flag and puts up the white one.

Our heads are high as we march to chow. Our voices are strong as we call the cadence. During Red Phase the drill sergeants just said, "Left . . . left . . . left, right, left . . ."

when we marched. In White Phase they sing songs.

"Used to date a beauty queen!" yells the drill sergeant on our way to chow.

"Used to date a beauty queen!" we repeat, our left foots hitting the ground on "used" and "beauty."

"Now I date my M16!" yells the drill sergeant.

There are a million of these songs. Army cadences to keep us in step with one another. The sound of us singing with one another—that rumbling, unified sound—it makes us a team. It makes us believe in one another. It gives us faith.

The private next to me knows exactly how sore I am, how tired, and how worn out. He knows exactly what I'm going through. But our left and right feet step onto the ground at the same time. All the privates surrounding me are dress, right, dressed. I follow them and they follow me.

We keep one another going. We're all in this together. No matter what happens we have one another.

We are on our way to becoming soldiers.

//////////////////// **RELIEF** ////////////////////

In Iraq two things keep us going: one another and letters from home—our unmistakable signs of love and support. But not all the letters are from our families.

A box is delivered to our barracks from an elementary school in North Carolina. It contains Slim Jims, instant tea, instant coffee, Pringles, Gummi Worms, peppermints, caramels, and mixed salted peanuts. The box also contains hygiene products: body soap, shampoo, deodorant, baby wipes, ChapStick, moisturizer, and pocket-sized bottles of antibacterial hand sanitizer.

These items are so appreciated and so vital to our welfare. A package with true thought behind it means so much more than the people who sent it may ever know. It's not "Thank God, I was almost out of soap." We could easily walk to the PX at camp and pick up a bar of soap. It's the feeling we get from knowing we're thought of.

Our real home is on the other side of the world. We can't see the magnetic yellow ribbons, the patriotic signs on people's front lawns. We aren't in a parade. We forget. The war is in the way.

Bottom line is it's nice to get a little slap on the back once in a while.

The hygiene products are great. The food is appreciated. But the letters are the best part about packages sent from schools. The kids are the people we're here for. We're fighting for them and their future. We're tired of the nagging and debating that adults do so well. We don't care anymore. We know more, we've seen more, and we're just plain sick of their arguments. The kids don't write to us about their political views.

Call it ignorance. Call it naïve. Call it unrealistic.

We call it relief.

I see a folded piece of green construction paper. On the front, in black crayon, there's an awkwardly drawn trapezoid sitting on a lumpy conveyor belt. It's a second grader's rendition of a tank, and a smiling face wearing a World War II helmet sticks out of the top. The tank's cannon shoots a triangle across the length of the paper. I can tell the triangle is shot from the cannon because there are three bullet straight lines connecting the two.

At the top, in blue crayon, there is one word, SOLDIER. Perhaps the most adorable part is the fact that after the word *soldier*, there is a comma. It's unnecessary, but the comma's there because this child knows that when you address a letter, you put a comma after the name.

My name is Soldier, and this is the letter that was left on my bunk this evening.

It is not the first time. We've already had a few of these packages. Every time one comes, the cards get dispersed throughout the barracks, one for every soldier, and the food and hygiene products are put on a shelf in the common room.

I smile at the card and take off my body armor. I put down my weapon and unlace my boots. I take off my shirt and feel the cool air of the barracks dry the sweat on my back. I pick up the card and open it.

It wasn't folded straight down the middle, so its edges don't quite line up. On the left side of the card there is a big drawing of the American flag. A dozen blue stars in the upper left-hand corner are unsymmetrical, crooked: perfect.

The kid tried to use a white crayon for the stripes but hasn't yet learned that white crayon never works. Uneven, horizontal streaks of pale wax alternating with uneven, horizontal red lines form the rest of the flag. There are seven stripes. Underneath it a big red *U*, a waxy white *S*, and a dark blue *A*.

On the right side a message sums up everything the kid would ever want to know about me. In lopsided, misspelled words he writes,

> How is Irak? Is it hot there? I hope your ok. I think you are brave. I have a dog. He pees on the floor and maks my dad mad. Do you hav a dog? Are you a general or a captin?

The innocence behind this last question makes me chuckle. At the bottom, exactly how his teacher taught him, the kid writes, *Thank you. From, Dylan*

It's a touching card, and the corners of my eyes start to feel ticklish. But I don't cry. It's just a card. The gluey, pulpy smell of the construction paper reminds me of second grade. There's a war going on outside, and I'd give anything to be in second grade again. But I don't cry.

I read the last line one more time, and I touch the raised, waxy letters. *Thank you.* I'm amazed at how easy it is for a kid to say yet it seems so hard for adults. I'm amazed at how much courage it takes to say it and at the courageous young boy who said it.

I reread the card, making sure I didn't miss anything. Then I touch it again, feeling the love and innocence of one little boy.

I lie down on my bunk. The war will be there tomorrow. The only thing that matters tonight is this green piece of construction paper.

We call it relief.

////////////// **WAR MIRACLES** //////////////

War is dirty and disgusting. It's ugly at face value. But in hindsight, the magical aspects of war are so obvious. And the miraculous thing, really, is that you missed them the first time.

Shortly before April I tell my family via e-mail that I'll be leaving on a month-long mission to a place that is famous. As always there's the OPSEC. I can't reveal the location even if I want to. But it's fun to tell them this way, to tug on their heartstrings a little. I can picture my mom scratching her head at the computer trying to figure out why I would refer to somewhere in Iraq as famous.

In April 2004, exactly one year ago, the American press was loaded with the first real scandal of the war. Pictures of Iraqi prisoners bound up and tied to leashes. American soldiers holding the other ends of these leashes, parading around these half-naked, sometimes fully naked, people. And one now-famous PFC in front of one naked prisoner. A bag over the prisoner's head and the PFC with a smile and thumbs-up for the camera.

All of this happened at Abu Ghraib prison.

When we arrive at the prison by a Chinook helicopter, we can tell right away that Abu Ghraib is a different world. It's the same war with the same fight, but there is something more: an aura of sorts.

It's an energy. This place is alive. Maybe some of it has to do with that whole naked photograph thing. Maybe its fame or infamy is what makes it so interesting, like Times Square in New York City. But there is something deeper. Just like the energy of New York City goes much deeper than Times Square.

For the next month ten soldiers from Headquarters Company will live the Abu Ghraib experience. We will breathe it and we will taste it.

There are several prison buildings on post, and we stay in one of the old ones. It's been converted from housing Iraqi prisoners to housing soldiers. A foot and a half of concrete protects us from the daily mortaring.

The base is small and personal, and I think this has a lot to do with its aura. The soldiers stationed at Abu Ghraib are the soldiers fighting the war. This is where the bad guys come to be punished. The genuine bad guys. Even the desk jockeys who live in Abu Ghraib aren't desk jockeys. They are investigators, interrogators, and intelligence. They run the war; it starts and ends with them.

In the chow hall we eat among top executives from the CID (Criminal Investigation Department) and the FBI. Romanian soldiers, who are allowed to have full beards, eat at the table across from us. Australian and British soldiers eat next to them. Most of the rest are either American military intelligence or MPs (Military Police). Some are KBR (Kellogg, Brown and Root) employees, which consist mostly of local Iraqis and "third country nationals" from places like India and the Philippines.

That's one thing people don't understand about this war. Everyone who hears "contractor" in relation to Iraq thinks it's some Halliburton or Blackwater rep who's pulling in $100,000 to $250,000 per year. People don't realize that the thousands of cooks, laundry service personnel, and shit/shower trailer cleaners who keep the war effort going are making about two hundred dollars a month. And that's their wage after they've reimbursed their companies for flying them to the theater. And guess where 100 percent of their wage goes. Not in their pockets. They send it home to support their families.

Perhaps the most fascinating group of soldiers at Abu

Ghraib is a small team of SF (Special Forces) who sit at the far table near the door. They don't talk to anyone. They don't have to. They wear the new uniforms that no one is yet issued: the gray and tan digital camouflage called the ACU (Army Combat Uniform). They don't wear rank or name tapes. There is only the strip on their left breast pocket, the pocket over their heart, that reads U.S. ARMY. Their pants aren't tucked in, and while off duty, they wear running sneakers instead of combat boots. Their hair is shaggy, their faces covered in stubble. They might shave once a week. Their eyes are dark and hold secrets that no one will ever know.

And we, like boys looking up to men, watch the SF guys from across the room. We respect them and fear them. But something in the darkness of their eyes says, "I respect you, too." Though I may just be imagining it.

This post has a life all its own. It's smack in the middle of a lush oasis. The surrounding palm trees give the impression of a jungle. It's like a different world, of wars past. It feels separated from the rest of Iraq.

Our engineering project is an earth-moving mission to flatten out the southeast corner of the base, thus making more room for prison space. Our operation is constantly delayed—sometimes for several minutes, sometimes for over an hour. All this delay for mortar attacks and car bombs: insurgents trying to break through and release their friends.

The regular hours are one of the most satisfying parts of this mission. We work seven A.M. to three P.M. with an hour for lunch at noon. There are two other engineering companies with whom we're working, and they handle the swing and night shifts. The days are hot and dusty, but the "union hours," as we call them, are heaven sent.

Also, our highest authority is two buck sergeants: Ken Payne and Tim Folden. Having a low-ranking command in the army is always a good thing. There are no higher-ups breathing down their necks to breathe down our necks about accountability or productivity. Work hours are leisurely and our activities off duty are less monitored.

There are eight of us besides Payne and Folden: Todd Wegner, Josh Roman, Justin Greene, Austin Rhodes, Josh Miller, and I, and two maintenance guys, Tomzack and Harding. Tomzack is a buck sergeant, and supervises Harding, a smart-ass specialist like the rest of us. Harding keeps an inflatable sheep in his room back at camp. The sheep has a hole built in underneath its tail. That's the kind of humor you see in the army.

The EQ guys, we run the dump trucks, dozers, graders, and the HYEX (Hydraulic Excavator). One of us sits in the HYEX on the northeast side of post. There's a giant surplus of dirt there. Two at a time, we drive dump trucks to the pick-up spot, the HYEX fills us up, and we drive to the southeast corner to dump. This is where we need to build up the land to make it level. As the dirt comes, we level it out with the dozers. Then, we fine-tune the leveling with the graders.

We take turns on the equipment, and Payne and Folden supervise. Tomzack and Harding wait for stuff to break down.

One morning around six thirty, we're sitting around the prison cell waking up. Josh Roman walks in from outside. He's an early bird today and went to breakfast chow. Abu Ghraib, by the way, has one of the best army chow halls I've ever eaten in. I think it's because KBR never has to cook for more than one thousand people. Breakfast is especially good, but only Roman went today.

We have a pot of coffee ready, and Folden pours us all cups. Roman grounds his rifle, Kevlar, and body armor.

"You guys hear the car bomb that went off this morning?" he asks. "Like six o'clock?"

No one had. Our prison building is less than a hundred yards from the front gate, apparently where it went off, and no one heard it. By April we're fully accustomed to explosions. We'd lived through Samarra and a couple explosions on the road, and Camp Anaconda was blown up regularly enough that an explosion meant little more than an inconvenient stay in a concrete bunker. When you're at war, a lot of things are on your mind. Worrying about every little thing that blows up is a waste of time. Besides, if a mortar or other kind of explosion is close enough to harm you, you're pretty much toasted no matter what. Most of the time it's unavoidable. Not to mention we were living in a concrete prison designed to confine terrorists. Not much could be heard through the walls of this place.

But Josh Roman sticks to his story. A car bomb went off a half an hour ago, and we should probably hold up a minute or two before going out to the job site. We continue to drink coffee and get ready. We put our tops on, lace up our boots, don our body armor, throw on our Kevlars, and grab our rifles. We are tentative. We calculate the odds of a second attack, but we have a mission.

In our prison-turned-barracks a short hallway where our prison rooms are located runs into the main hallway. The main hallway leads outside. On the ceiling of the main hallway, every twenty or so feet, there are long fluorescent lights. The hallway's walls are solid concrete except for spots of built-in ventilation that let in a quarter inch of dust from the sandstorms.

In the winter in Iraq you get peanut butter mud. The rest of the year sandstorms throw around enough dust to bury Manhattan.

I walk down our little hallway.

"I'm telling you, man, don't go out there," says Roman. "They're hot today."

Where our little hallway meets the main hallway, I turn

around and in the coolest voice I say, "Ah, Roman, quit bein' a pussy."

As I turn around—

Ka-blam!

—a second car bomb explodes.

It's funny how intuitive your body can be to violent explosions. After only a handful of them you can tell how far away, what direction, and even a rough estimate of the size. This one is huge, and it comes from the main gate.

The percussion blast, even through the thick concrete walls, numbs my brain for a second. I watch as the layer of dust on the floor jumps into the air and settles back down as if it's connected. A single dirt blanket. Like magic.

One of the fluorescent lights unhinges and swings down from one side. One of the light tubes pops out, flies through the air, and shatters in a white cloud of dust. The other tube sits in the swinging housing flickering on and off, trying to stay lit.

I pivot a ballet-worthy 180 degrees and tell Roman, "I think we should wait a little while. They're hot today."

Nowhere else could that timing have been better. And nowhere else can you find humility in the form of a car bomb.

After a good half hour we walk to the job site and begin working. It's just another day.

* * *

On another day Todd Wegner runs from a mortar attack.

Miller, Roman, and I hear the mortars go off as we deal out a game of Texas Hold 'Em. Playing poker is an excellent way to kill time in the army.

I wave a hand to the room across the hall. "Hey, Sergeant Folden!" I yell.

"Yeah?"

"We're not dead," I say.

"That's good," he says.

After any attack we have to report to our chain of command that we're okay. This is called accountability.

"Are you all in there?" Folden asks me.

"Except Wags."

"All right."

And we continue our game. We're using these awful candies for poker chips. They come from a big bowl in the chow hall, and no one ever eats them. Remember the sugar-free candies you get after a good checkup at the dentist? They're worse than those.

We each grabbed a healthy handful on our way back from dinner chow. No one thought to bring poker chips with us to Abu Ghraib, and they were the next best thing. They come in four colors, and we give each color a value. Red is five, orange is ten, yellow is twenty, and green is a hundred.

Mortars are flying around exploding, and Josh Roman raises my bet.

"I'm going to beat you like the Red Sox beat the Yankees," he says.

"Low blow, man. Low blow."

Roman is from Massachusetts. I'm from New York. His room back at Anaconda is kitty-corner to mine. So when I walk out of my room, I have to see his stupid 2004 World Series championship banner he hung on his wall outside. On my wall outside, I wrote, "Yeah, 1 out of 86 ain't bad." Then, just to one-up him, I stole a pair of his underwear (clean underwear, thank you) and wrote "Go, Yankees" down the fly in permanent marker.

I see his raise, and then the son of a bitch throws down a full house. Then he collects the pile of dentist candy.

Josh Miller, from Nowhere, Ohio, grew up on a dairy farm. He says he's thankful he folded.

Then Todd Wegner runs into our room. He's out of breath and sweating.

"Holy shit," he says.

He's smiling, thankful to be alive, I suppose.

"What happened to you?" I ask him.

"Did you hear those mortars?"

"Yeah."

"I was just running from them," he says. "Holy shit, man. That was crazy."

There's a wooden rack in the common area where we place our Kevlars, body armor, and weapons. It's our best friend at three o'clock, when our shift ends.

Todd is sweating bullets and heaving like he just finished a PT test. He was on his way back from this Internet café, and he ran all the way from the middle of the base to our barracks. He doesn't even acknowledge the existence of the rack, just stands there smiling, in shock. I ask him if he wants in on some poker, and all he says is "Holy shit."

On his face is another story. He wants to say much more. He wants to grab us and shake us into reality. He wants us to understand, to feel his fear, his excitement, the high he is on. We simply can't.

"Hey, Folden!" I yell. "Wags is here."

"All right!" he yells back. "Good to see you, buddy."

"Want us to deal you in?" I ask again.

"Yeah, yeah," he says, his mind still wrapping around the fact that he has just run from flying bombs.

"All right. Blind is ten," I say, and deal.

"Holy shit," Wegner says to himself. His hands are shaking as he puts his gear on the rack.

A few days later I leave the barracks to grab some dinner. I go alone because it's nice to have solitude sometimes.

Abu Ghraib is a unique setup for a military post because it was a high security prison. It has a series of small secure bases inside one larger secure base. The inner sections are mostly housing quarters, command quarters, and the main prison buildings. The chow hall and Internet/phone café are large trailers in the middle of all these tiny enclosed bases.

The enclosed section in which we're staying has a barracks, a laundry service station, and a gym with free weights, treadmills, and machines. It's surrounded by a twenty-foot-high concrete wall with guard towers. When the guard towers are manned, it means things have gone horribly awry. At the entrance to our section there's a spot where a manned gate once stood, but there is no longer a need for one. Our "gate" is now a thirty-foot break in the wall.

As I near the break in the wall, thinking about the day, it's close to the end of dinner chow, and no one is around.

My rifle is slung across my back. For the first weeks in-country it was hard to get used to the awkwardness of body armor. One of the difficulties was taking my weapon on and off. Its sling got caught on my ammo pouches, tourniquet, bayonet, field dressing pack, or my arm. By now, though, I am used to the mechanics of protective clothing and could probably pull my weapon across my armored body while shimmying underneath a dump truck and eating Twinkies. I've strategically shifted the components attached to my armor so there is a diagonal stretch of open body armor where my sling fits snug.

Right outside of our gate is the post's fuel point: two M978 HEMTT trucks that each hold 2,500 gallons of diesel fuel. Any piece of equipment on post that needs fuel comes here. It's nice having the fuel point so close to us. That is except for one minor detail: five thousand gallons of diesel fuel is one hell of a target for mortar attacks.

A bird flies over my head, a very fast bird, nothing more than a dark streak. And it's flying too low. The sound catches up, and I realize this is no bird. A deep gust follows the dark streak over my head. Then the bird explodes about thirty yards away, near the helipad. The helipad is another big target for the attacks. To destroy its flat surface is to hinder the ability for helicopters to land.

Smoke and debris fly downward over the helipad. The explosion resonates through my bones, and I see what kind of mortar this is: the most dangerous kind, an airburst.

Impact mortars explode when they hit something. But the problem with those is that, unless the mortar is right on target, half the shrapnel is embedded into the ground.

The airburst mortar that flies over my head attempts to solve the problem of wasted shrapnel. Probably this one uses a radio frequency. Inside the mortar round is a little micro-transmitter that sends out a continuous radio signal. As the mortar sends and receives the signal, sort of like a bat flying blind, it knows how far off the ground it is. At a predetermined measurement, usually about ten feet, the round explodes. And what you get is 100 percent of the shrapnel flying into your target.

The explosion barely breaks my stride. I am going to

chow, and that's where I plan on being in a couple minutes. When bombs go off on a convoy, our SOP is to push through, just keep driving no matter what. This reaction is less about survival than it is about control. Truth is I have no control over a roadside bomb or IED. I have no control over whether or not an airburst mortar round lands on my head. But I do have control over whether or not I run.

Up until this point mortars are nothing more than a nuisance. If we are outside and hear explosions, we have to stop, find shelter, and wait out the attack. Mortar attacks just annoy me. They make me feel like a prisoner.

But today I'm not going to be made a prisoner by this flying bomb. I am going to dinner, for God's sake. I have never been close enough to a mortar to hear the deep gush of it flying before it explodes. It's a startling whoosh, a quick displacement of air, and then the boom of the explosion.

I keep walking, about to get to the gate. I hope I get to see another one explode just so it will make for a better story. But that probably won't happen. They usually don't launch a second one. And they almost never launch more than two. These munitions, they're costly.

Whoosh, whoosh; BOOM, BOOM. I get my wish.

Two of them, side by side. I can't see them, but these explosions are even louder than the explosions from the first one. I can feel the ground shake. *They are close, just the other side of the wall,* I think. Five thousand gallons of diesel fuel—that's

37,750 pounds—sit on the other side of the wall.

It's time to swallow my pride and run.

Whoosh; BOOM.

Another bird, way too fast for a normal bird.

I am a hundred yards away from my barracks, and I turn a quick circle looking for a closer refuge.

"You know where you are?" a soldier yells to me over the last explosion. He's twenty yards away and sees the confusion on my face. All his weight is on one foot, ready to take off toward his barracks. He wants to make sure I am okay before he runs, because that's what soldiers do. That's how we stay alive.

I shake my head and yell, "No!"

"Follow me," he says.

Whoosh; BOOM.

And I don't argue.

He runs around the side of the nearest building to what appears to be a sort of alleyway. He runs past a closed door and continues around the far side of the building.

What's wrong with that door? I wonder.

Whoosh; BOOM.

This mortar lands behind me aways. The ground shakes. Think being chased by a T. Rex.

Where will the next one land? I wonder.

My guide runs along a chain-link fence that stretches between two barracks buildings: converted prisons. He runs toward the fence's open gate. Here, the dirt runs into gravel, and his feet slip beneath him.

Whoosh; BOOM.

He goes down. If I didn't know better, I would reach for my field dressing or tourniquet. The timing for him to slip on the gravel couldn't have been better. It's almost comical the way it happens. The way he falls at the perfect moment, as though he's slid into home plate just as the ball lands in the catcher's mitt, just as the flying bomb lands in Abu Ghraib. It's magical the way it happens.

I catch up to him quickly.

"You—"

Whoosh; BOOM.

"You okay?" I yell as I grab the handle on the back of his body armor.

"Yeah," he says as I help him to his feet. "Come on."

I follow him to a nearby enclosed stairwell. His quarters are at the top of the stairs. The standard waiting time after an attack is twenty minutes.

Whoosh; BOOM.

Twenty minutes.

A handful of his friends are hanging out in the common area. We talk while we wait. They are Navy. Something to do with intelligence. The guy who led me here is a petty officer, the equivalent of a sergeant in the army. I ask him about the war and about his mission. He asks me about ours. We talk about the army and the navy and about Abu Ghraib. When things are safe, I thank him, shake his hand, and head back to my barracks.

When I get back, I want to grab my friends and shake them into understanding the fear, the excitement, the high I am on. I want to share it.

Todd Wegner, he's from outside of Dallas. He smiles and nods. He asks me if I want to be dealt in. I say yes. And Josh Roman, who's a damn Red Sox fan, wins another hand with a full house. Josh Miller, who grew up milking cows, is thankful he folded.

I see the petty officer in the chow hall from time to time. We say hi, nothing too intimate. But that's the way it is, the way it has to be. Like magic.

When we leave Abu Ghraib and head back to Anaconda, he might have wondered, "What ever happened to that kid from the army?" *Now you see me, now you don't.* He helped me when I needed to find cover, and I picked him up when he fell.

We were even.

Shortly after the ten of us get back from Abu Ghraib, Munoz gives me the best news he's given me all tour.

"Smithson, you got the May leave you wanted," he says.

If this wasn't the army, I'd kiss him.

See, the army is unfair and unreliable in a lot of ways. Think of the two months I waited to hear if I was being deployed. Think of a commander who cares more about his Humvee being clean than the guy who drives it. But the army is also, sometimes, very understanding and generous.

During a combat tour the army lets us go home for a

two-week "leave." Since we have missions still going on in Iraq, the unit has to divide the leave slots over the course of about eight months. Every two weeks, a handful of soldiers from the company take their leave.

To keep everything fair, the company has a lottery. The order in which we are picked is the order in which we choose the slot we want.

I chose May for a couple reasons. It would probably be right in the middle of the tour. And May 19 is Heather and my unofficial anniversary. It was our first date: her junior prom.

So when I get back from Abu Ghraib and Munoz gives me the good news, I call Heather and my parents. I tell them I'm coming home. My heart beats through my chest, and I ride on clouds for the next week as I wait for my date to fly out.

Think of this two-week leave as a build-up. Think White Phase.

Another great thing about going on leave is that, because I have to be at camp in order to fly out, Munoz and LT won't be sending me on any missions. I do the normal PMCS, cleaning the barracks, busy work. But I don't have any outside-the-wire missions during which something might go wrong or something might hold us up and cause me to miss my flight.

The PAX (Passenger Terminal) is a series of tan tents

where soldiers wait to fly out of Anaconda. The thing about moving soldiers is there are a lot of them. There are hundreds of soldiers waiting at the PAX terminal. The air force planes flying in and out of Anaconda are capable of fitting only so many people in addition to running other missions.

We're more or less hitching a ride. And the cargo, supplies, and personnel for the aircrafts' missions take precedence over soldiers going on leave.

Long story short, the PAX terminal works like this:

We're given an ETD (Estimated Time of Departure). The ETD approaches, but no one shows up to take us to our flight. A couple hours go by, and we're given a new ETD. There is a mechanical problem or the aircraft was bumped to another mission or there's cargo taking up space that they didn't originally expect. So we have to wait for the next flight.

I haven't talked to a single soldier who's flown out of the PAX terminal on their first ETD. Don't get me wrong, though. I'd rather be killing time on the wooden floor of the PAX terminal than running around outside the wire any day. It's not hard to keep life in perspective when you're in a combat zone. All you have to do is bring a good book or a deck of cards and waiting at the PAX terminal is no big deal.

After two and a half days of getting our ETD pushed

back, we grab our stuff, throw it onto a large pallet, and pack onto a giant C130.

This military cargo plane is designed so that supplies, equipment, and vehicles (including vehicles as large as tanks) can fit down the middle. And running along each side of the aircraft's interior are fold-down seats for passengers. So when the air force has a logistics mission to fly cargo out of Iraq and to Kuwait, some soldiers and a couple pallets of their stuff can hitch a ride.

We land in Camp Doha, Kuwait, where our vehicles and equipment came off the navy ships, and we spend the night in tents. In the tent it's easy to spot the guys who are used to living out of their rucksacks. Certain soldiers, especially those with infantry unit patches, have bags and gear all covered in dirt and dust. They move through the cramped, efficiently packed bags like they've done it a thousand times. The same way you can tell new sneakers from old sneakers, you can tell the guys who've been traveling around Iraq.

And there are other soldiers with squeaky clean Kevlars and body armor. The green straps on their rucksacks are still stiff and crimped from being adjusted recently. They're usually officers. They're finance workers, or mail clerks, or members of some battalion staff, planning team somewhere. They have very necessary jobs, I'm sure, just not very dangerous ones.

I look around the tent, my hand fishing through my rucksack for my toothbrush, and I feel a sense of resentment toward these clean, inexperienced soldiers. I don't know if it's because I'm jealous or because I'm full of myself. Somehow, just knowing that there are soldiers in Iraq who don't have to deal with death, who sit in offices and don't worry about never returning to their families, I don't know, it just makes me mad. It makes me feel like they don't deserve to go on leave, like they should volunteer it for the soldiers who aren't so lucky.

But, really, I'm too tired to care. I've been napping in between reading and eating and waiting for the next ETD push-back. That kind of schedule is exhausting. I brush my teeth at the shower trailers and go to sleep.

The next day we line up in formation, throw our stuff on pallets, hand in our body armor for until we return, and board a plane out of Kuwait. After fueling up in Germany, we take off for a hop over the Atlantic.

When the pilot announces that you can see the coast of the United States, every window cover slides up, and this plane full of tired soldiers still wearing our DCUs (Desert Combat Uniforms), that wavy tan-and-brown camouflage, turns into a roomful of kids on Christmas morning.

We land in Raleigh, North Carolina, and the pilot says, "Welcome home."

Everyone in the plane claps and cheers. For most of

us North Carolina isn't our home, but it's a hell of a lot closer than Iraq. And being on American soil is like living a dream.

The soldiers disperse in the large airport, and only one other soldier and I go to the gate for the plane heading to Albany, New York. She sits down on the other side of the waiting area, and I realize that she's from my old unit in Kingston.

On the plane the pilot has open seats in first class, and since we're in uniform, he lets us sit there. If it were up to me, I'd sit in the middle of the plane like everyone else. And people would treat me the way they've always treated me, like I'm just another passenger on the plane. When you're traveling in uniform, especially a desert uniform, all you want is anonymity.

But the pilot makes a big deal of it, and people stare at the wavy tan-and-brown clothes I've been wearing since November. I move to the front seat and find the soldier from my old unit sitting there. I'm glad to be flying next to her. Throughout this whole leave experience, I've been traveling with other soldiers. We've been jumping through military posts, and no one there looked at me twice.

Now, back in the civilian world, the camouflage I'm wearing is anything but camouflage. I wish the army didn't make us travel in uniform. I wish this plane was filled with people who actually understand the war, not people who think that, because I'm in uniform, I want to talk about it.

Truth is I don't. And these people staring, they make me feel a whole lot of resentment I didn't know existed. I keep expecting the know-it-all who thinks I want to hear his opinion about the war. I keep expecting to hear those tired arguments, that "We don't belong in Iraq" and "Nothing good is happening over there" and "Bush is a moron" and all the rest of it.

I don't even want to think about Iraq. All I want to do is go home. Yet I know that because I'm in uniform some opinionated jerk-off is going to bombard me with his views like I care—like I had anything to do with the invasion of Iraq.

What would he want me to do, anyway? Say, "Yeah, I think you're right. Let me go tell my commander-in-chief and see if I can turn this thing around." Get real.

But luckily I don't meet this guy. In first class I sit with the only person on this plane who understands the war the same way I do: the soldier from my old unit.

"Hey," I say. "How have you been?"

"Good, you?" she says.

"Better now that I'm out of the desert. It's so nice to see grass and trees again."

"I know," she says. "Are you with an engineering unit?"

"Yeah. Are you?"

"No, I'm not an engineer. I was just in Kingston because

that's the closest unit that needed my MOS. I was cross-leveled to a postal unit."

"How is that?"

"It's really cool, actually," she says. "Being able to give people their mail, it's really rewarding. I guess that seems silly."

"Not at all. Mail is what keeps us going," I say. "You ever have to go outside the wire?"

"A couple times," she says. "My commander needed me to go on a few runs. Just around Baghdad and stuff. You?"

"Yeah, quite a bit," I say. "It gets old, living out of a rucksack all the time. But you get used to it."

"Have you lost anyone?" she asks me.

"No. Couple of close calls, little IEDs and stuff, but no casualties," I say. I almost forget to add, "Knock on wood."

"You're lucky," she says. "We haven't lost anyone from my unit, but I meet a lot of people at the post office, you know?"

"Sure."

"I was pretty close to this one guy," she says, her eyes getting distant. "He died two weeks ago. And another friend of mine died last month, right before he was supposed to go on leave. Can you believe it?"

I shake my head.

"He had a little girl," she says. "She was born while he was deployed."

"He never got to see her."

She shakes her head.

"I'm sorry," I say.

"It's hard," she says. "It's really hard."

There's a pain in her voice I can't relate to. She wipes a tear, and I wonder if she feels about me the way I felt about those sparkling clean officers and paperwork junkies in the tent in Kuwait. Maybe she feels like I don't deserve to go on leave. Maybe she feels like I can't understand her experiences the way I feel like the civilians on this plane can't understand mine.

When our plane lands in Albany International, the pilot lets us off first. The whole plane claps for us, and I shake the pilot's hand.

"Thank you," I say.

"No, thank you," he says.

The soldier and I walk down the tunnel together, out of the throat that swallowed us on our way to Iraq.

Airport security allows our families to meet us at the gate. Heather and my parents are standing there.

"See you in two weeks," says the other soldier as we separate.

She walks toward her husband and daughter.

"You too," I say. "Enjoy it."

I walk to Heather first, and kissing her, I realize I forgot how sweet her lips taste. We stand holding each other, and right now, nothing else matters. I am right where I need to be.

"I missed you so much," she whispers, laying her head on my shoulder.

"I missed you, too," I say.

"Happy anniversary," she says.

I check my digital watch. She's right. It's the nineteenth.

"Wow, I didn't even realize," I say, kissing her again. "Happy anniversary."

"Well, you did just fly through, what, eight time zones?"

"Yeah. That tends to mess you up."

I let her go and hug my parents.

"Oh, I missed you, Ryan," says my mom.

"Glad to see you, pal," says my dad. "How was the flight?"

"Long," I say.

We walk through the airport, and I tell them about the other soldier on the plane, how she is from my old unit. I don't tell them about the fallen soldiers she knows.

When we get to the security checkpoint, I see the rest of the family. Some of Heather's family is there, including her sister's daughter, my niece, who was born the day I flew to Fort Bragg. This is the first time I've seen her, and she is adorable.

I look into her large blue eyes and say, "Hi, Sophia. I'm Uncle Ryan."

I think of the other soldier on the plane. I think of her friend who never got to see his baby. Almost without trying, I shut out the thought and give hugs to the rest of the family.

My sister is graduating from high school this year, and my parents hold a party for her at their house. They plan it for the weekend I am home. I feel a little guilty taking the spotlight off my sister, but it's nice to see all those aunts, uncles, and extended family.

The weather the day of the party is warm and sunny. There are balloons tied to the edge of the patio and a grill cooking hot dogs. There are people throwing Frisbees and playing horseshoes. People eating, laughing, and spending time together. And my parents' dog, a golden retriever named Haley, is begging the guests for food.

She slipped a disk in her lower spine about a year ago, and her back half became paralyzed. But Haley is still her happy old self. She runs—well, stumbles—around the party looking for food and trying to chase the Frisbee.

My dad recently finished the back room in his garage. It was a horse stable when we moved here in 1994. But he just finished making it a "man's corner" for the party. It has a dartboard and a foosball table. It also has a poker table and a fridge for beer.

I walk up the driveway toward the entrance to the garage. I plan on playing some darts.

One thing that really sucks about being home on leave from Iraq is that you have to go back. No matter how hard you try, the thoughts of Iraq never wash out of your mind. I can leave Iraq, but Iraq can never leave me.

As I near the entrance of the garage, I hear a gunshot.

The way I stop moving every muscle of my body, it's like Haley must have felt when she slipped that disk. I hunch down and tighten my fists. My forehead sweats, and my eyes dart around. I look all over my parents' backyard for the silhouette of a man running, or the muzzle flash of an AK-47, or a mushroom cloud. Adrenaline feels like needles when it pumps through your veins. It's a feeling I'm so used to in Iraq that here it seems so far out of place it's scary.

This isn't supposed to be scary. This is my parents' house. This is safe.

"What was that?" I ask anyone who can hear me. The closest person is my dad, twenty feet away, and he's laughing.

"Seriously, what was that?" I ask again.

I hear anger in my voice. I hear all the people at the party. It's the sound of an Iraqi village. I swear, somewhere in the clash of voices, somewhere among these party guests laughing and spending time together, I swear there's someone speaking Arabic.

"It was a balloon, Ryan. It popped," my dad says,

laughing some more. "You okay?"

His voice is distant, like he's speaking through a tunnel. Like he's eight hours away.

"Yeah, yeah," I say, taking a deep breath. "I'm fine."

I walk into the garage, but before I get to the back room, I take a minute to calm down. The cool, still air of the garage is comforting. That smell of old oil and grass clippings, it assures me that I'm safe. The Peg-Board of tools on the back wall and the canoe hanging in the rafters, they remind me that I'm home. Safe.

The back room is cramped with people. I don't stay long. I don't play darts. I grab a drink and go to the back corner of the yard.

Heather and her sister are there watching Sophia roll around on a blanket. My sister, Regan, and her best friend are poking at the fire pit, talking about the upcoming summer. I kiss Heather on the forehead and take a seat in an open fold-out chair.

"When are we going out of town?" I ask.

"Two days," Heather says. "You okay? You look upset."

"A balloon popped."

She nods her head. Her sister looks at me funny.

"It's okay," says Heather. "Just a balloon."

"I know."

Two days later, she and I take a trip to Manchester, Vermont. It's our special getaway for the two weeks. It's our alone time, our anniversary. We book a nice dinner at a fine French restaurant. She wears a short black-and-white dress and I wear a three-piece suit. She straightens her brunette hair and I, well, I'm practically bald.

We stay in a bed-and-breakfast just outside of town and go shopping during the day. It's the middle of the week so there are no crowds. Perfect for me.

"How are you doing?" asks Heather as we watch the fake fireplace in our room.

"I'm all right," I say.

"You sure? You don't really seem yourself."

"Yeah, I'm fine."

"It's not me, is it?"

"No, babe. Not at all," I say, pulling her close. "It's just weird to be home."

"Yeah, I know."

"I mean, just a couple weeks ago, I was in Abu Ghraib."

"Yeah," she says. "That mission went okay though, right?"

"It went fine, it's just . . ." I say.

"Just what?"

She doesn't need to know about the mortars. Or the kids in Samarra. It will just worry her.

"It's just," I say, "I worry. You know, about the other guys. I feel like I should be there with them."

"Yeah," she says. "But I like you here with me."

"Me too."

We kiss, and I try so hard to keep this moment forever.

"Plus," she says, climbing on top of me, "the other guys can't give you this."

Fifteen days go way too fast. No matter how hard I try to hold on to the moment, it comes and goes.

The day before I leave we move from our little apartment in Troy to a large apartment in West Sand Lake. It's a quaint little town between the suburbs and the country. It has a little corner grocery store and gas station, an elementary school the size of an ice rink, and a barbershop with a sign that says, NO APPOINTMENT NEEDED.

On the way to the airport the ride is silent. My parents drive their car, and Heather and I drive in hers.

We pull into a parking spot, and Heather turns the car off. Me in my desert camouflage, and all our stuff left packed in boxes at the new apartment. Boxes she'll have to unpack herself. I'm abandoning her again.

"Sorry I can't help you unpack," I say.

"You helped," she says. "We got everything moved in."

"I know. I just feel like . . . like I'm leaving you behind with all this work. And I'm not going to be here to help you. I feel like—"

"Ryan," she says, taking my hand, "I want you to know how proud I am of you. It means so much to me that you're strong enough to defend your country. I couldn't ask for a better husband."

I don't say anything. I pull her close and kiss her. With our eyes closed the feeling of our lips together is deeper than ever. We stay connected, touching each other, just hoping it will last a little longer.

I feel her chin start to quiver against mine. I keep kissing her, trying so hard to stay strong, trying so hard to hold on to this moment.

Of all the good-byes the army has made me say, this is the hardest. I've made it for six months in a combat zone. I've gotten a little taste of home: Heather's sweet lips. And I keep denying that this may be our last good-bye.

"I love you so much," she says, pulling back. She looks into my eyes like no one else ever could. I wipe the tears off her cheek.

"I love you, too," I say.

"Only a few more months."

"Stay strong, honey."

"You too."

We get out of the car and walk to the airport. As we make our way through the security check, there's a TV showing the weather and news. There's a story about Iraq. I don't pay attention, but I see the brown desert. I see the soldiers walking through it. I remember my brothers and one sister still over there, still running missions and waiting for me to come back.

At the gate I see the soldier I flew home with. As if

looking into a mirror, I can see on her face that desperation of trying to stop time. On the wall a digital clock marks the seconds going by. People sit all around us, other passengers waiting to go on vacation or business trips. People going to visit family—using the same plane I'm using to leave my family behind.

There's such a look of pity on these people's faces when they see my desert uniform, when they see my family's tears. I can see it on their faces, that apologetic look wishing they could do something. But they can't. And neither can I.

And there's the last call to board.

I hug my parents and kiss them good-bye. They tell me they love me and that they're proud of me. I get to kiss Heather one last time and then walk away, abandoning her.

Unpacked boxes. Unfinished business.

The soldier from Kingston, she sits in the window seat. I sit in the aisle. First class, like it matters. Most of the ride back to Iraq is silent.

///// SATAN'S CLOTHES DRYER /////

When I return, it's the beginning of June. The Iraqi summer is in full swing. Coming back isn't so bad. Getting on the plane in Albany was the hardest part. In Kuwait when I was given back my body armor, I almost welcomed the transition to something familiar.

I'm on a lumber hauling mission up to Bravo Company at Q-West. SFC Morrow is my assistant driver (A-driver) in an M916 tractor trailer. Hauling supplies and equipment, the army calls this logistics. When we convoy for a logistics mission, it's called a Logistics Package, or LOGPAC.

A LOGPAC is one of the many single-day missions we conduct as Headquarters Company. Sometimes things go wrong and we don't get out in one day. Sometimes we have to stay for a couple days. This is why we always pack extra socks and a toothbrush. This is why we're so used to living out of our rucksacks.

The full name of Q-West is Qayyarah West. It's a town outside of Mosul, near the border of Turkey. Soldiers call it Q-West because it sounds like Key West, the coastal paradise in Florida. It's this sarcasm that really keeps us going. It's the little things. Like zombie Whisler. Or sugar-free dentist candy for poker chips. It's a two-week taste of home.

In Q-West there's an army camp where B Company stays. It's called FOB (Forward Operating Base) Endurance, and it usually takes five solid hours to get there. Five hours of bone-dry desert, no scenery whatsoever. The earth is monotonous brown. The sky is tinted tan. The buildings are few and far between, and even they are the crumbly brown of dried mud. Any plants, which are also few and far between, are the pathetic shade of a dead lawn after the spring thaw.

The road to Q-West is usually very long and very uninspiring. But not today. Today we're witnessing a new variation of the only color in Iraq. It's a living, breathing, translucent brown.

In Iraq, especially in the northern region during summer, dust devils are rampant. On a camp like Anaconda where there are buildings and mortar barriers that block the wind, the dust devils are tiny. The dirt gets caught in the corner of a building, and it turns into a little devil, dancing around like a child until the breeze stops blowing for a second. Then it fizzles out.

But today, out in the open desert, the dust devils resemble skyscrapers. They stand hundreds of feet in the air and are as wide as a city block.

Really, it's funny how much there is to a country that you can't see while standing right in it. I've never seen more than one of these giant dust devils at a time before. But today the sand gray horizon resembles the final scene in the movie *Twister*. The dust devils are enormous and everywhere. No less than four at any given time.

Even when they rise and fall, like a changeover between movie scenes, the dust devils are never gone.

The dust is in my boots and on my eyelashes. It sticks to my sweat and soaks up my urine. It's in the food I eat, the letters I write, and the dreams I have. But the collections of the dust, the true devils, they eventually dissolve.

One of the many grand beasts flies sideways across the open desert. It comes from the right toward the road. The M916 ahead of us, which is about one hundred and fifty meters away, narrowly avoids it. The mischievous devil runs across the road just after the tractor trailer passes. The giant wall of dirt blocks the entire road, and I can no longer see the first half of the convoy.

"Whoa, ho-ho!" I say. "Hold on!"

"Smithson," says Morrow.

He sounds like he's warning me. He doesn't know whether to be scared or excited. This unsure apprehension, it's the one constant in Iraq. A constant inconsistency: it's part of the combat experience. It's never really a "fight or flight" dilemma. This is a war, after all. There's no point in running. Face the truth. Face the devil.

Overcoming the fear of the unknown is the ultimate rush. I grip the wheel and hold on with white knuckles. We are only hauling lumber, so the load isn't very heavy. We're traveling about sixty miles per hour and mistakes are lethal at that speed.

We blast through the first wall of dark dirt. Our small, dictionary-sized armored windows are open to allow for ventilation. Ventilation is more than what we get. The dust swirls around inside the cab. Little pieces of rock hit my face and bounce off my Kevlar. Morrow grips the "oh shit" handle in front of him and doesn't say a word.

All I see is brown dirt. All I see is Iraq. A massive circle surrounds us and slowly rotates. We are inside Satan's clothes dryer. We're in the middle of Iraq on Highway 1, the main service route that runs up the middle of the country. It's also called MSR (Main Service Route) Tampa. But what we call it doesn't matter, because right now it doesn't exist. We're in the middle of nowhere in a swirling cloud of dirt. And all we can see is the cab of this 916 and each other.

This devil surrounds us. Like a front sight post set in the middle of a rear aperture, we're surrounded on all sides by this out-of-focus delirium that is war. We learn how impossibly big the world is and how impossibly small we are. We learn that situations, our reactions to them, and the results that follow are all just micro-level nonsense. We are so insignificant. This country engulfs us. It's so beyond what we can see.

We think of safety and comfort. Because nothing can reach us here. We think of fear and death. Because we can reach nothing from here. We have lustful thoughts of what we'll do to our wives when we return home. Regretful thoughts of what we've done to our wives, who now sleep alone. Hearts are beating and sweat pores leaking.

Morrow grips his M203. I grip the steering wheel. I'm checking my mirrors. He's checking his faith. My eyes blink and my tongue wets my lips.

I notice the lack of pull on the vehicle. Apparently, appearances are deceiving. The giant devil was no more a threat to us than the wind through which we drive every day. I begin laughing as the second wall of dark dirt comes at us—or we come at it. Dust and small rocks invade our small cabin space once again. The dust sticks to the sweat on my face, the moisture on my lips, and my laughter increases.

We emerge from the dust devil, and the rest of the convoy comes back into focus. The rest of Iraq is visible. We are freed, temporarily unfettered, I tip my head back and laugh toward the ceiling. It's a laugh of relief, the laugh that conquers the devil. He is behind us, and all I want to do is fall down laughing.

I look to Morrow, who seems less amused at our successful run with the devil. I think he may have squirted a small amount of butt chocolate, and I laugh harder.

"Oh my God," I say. "Did you see that?"

"Jesus," he says, and shakes his head.

"Did you see that?" I laugh harder. "That was fuckin' awesome!"

"Yeah," he says. "Jesus."

//////// 9/29/04

Heather and I looking fantastic on our wedding night at Buca Di Beppo restaurant.

///////// 12/24/04 /////////

SPC Austin Rhodes and I at Camp Scania during the three-day push from Kuwait to Iraq.

Members of EQ platoon celebrate the New Year by squatting in a mortar bunker for an hour. I am second from right.

SPC Justin Greene poses with an Iraqi boy on the bridge/
farmland restoration mission.

Many units paint murals on the concrete barriers scattered throughout Camp Anaconda. These two provide both protection for the Air Force chow hall and the once-in-a-lifetime opportunity to catch the three superheroes of Iraq in one photograph.

Driving a dump truck in Abu Ghraib while wearing, of course, aviator sunglasses.

Jerkface perches on my finger . . . and totally hogs the camera.

1LT Andrew Zeltwanger receives his own pair of aviator sunglasses in the mail . . . and then goes around intimidating everyone.

Almost near the end of the tour and more than ready to go home, members of EQ platoon pose on a Humvee in FOB Wilson. From left to right: SPC Todd Wegner, SSG Robert Gasparotto, SPC Austin Rhodes, SPC Steven Hirth, SPC Jesse Smith, myself, SGT Marc Zerega, SPC Justin Greene, SGT Chris Dreager.

////////////// HARD CANVAS //////////////

"**W**hat do we got today?" asks Ryan Ludwin.

He's poking around inside two Styrofoam to-go plates from the chow hall. They're full of oranges, apples, and grapes. They're full of silver-dollar pancakes and small packets of syrup. They're full of bite-sized breakfast sandwiches and bacon and sausage. They sit beside boxes of orange juice, grapefruit juice, and fruit punch, which are all covered in Arabic writing.

It's 5:45 A.M., and the to-go plates sit on the hood of our Humvee. We're all half asleep, sipping coffee and munching breakfast. Tom Skavenski, our gunner, walks across the motor pool with his M60 machine gun. Ken Renninger, my A-driver, comes by, a Marlboro Red in his hand. He takes a drag, pats me on the back, and thanks me for grabbing breakfast.

"How are we this morning, Smitty?" he asks.

"Pretty good, Sarge," I say. "Ready for another day?"

"Yep," he says as he grabs a sausage-egg-and-cheese on an English muffin.

I'm the driver of this Humvee, bumper number H-105, and only I have the keys. So early in the morning, shortly after the chow hall opens, I drive down, pick up breakfast for my crew, and bring it back to the barracks. It isn't really one of my duties, but I feel it's important to have a full stomach before we head out.

In the middle of the day, no matter how hungry we are, it's hard to eat. It usually hovers around 125 degrees in this part of Iraq, and when it's that hot, your stomach wants only water. Anything else feels sickening.

There are three other Humvees in this convoy and an M916 hauling concrete supplies. They're parked throughout the front of the barracks. Their drivers, gunners, and A-drivers are loading gear, water, and ammo. I follow Skavenski to the ammo shed, where he pulls out four OD green boxes and gives me two of them. When we get back to the Humvee, I hand them up to him as he stands on our armored roof.

"So what did you get me for breakfast?" he asks.

"Spinach quiche and a Bloody Mary," I say.

"Nice," he says, laughing. "Remind me to pick you up a filet mignon later."

LT Zeltwanger rallies the briefing. We form up in a circle around him. It's still dark out, so he holds a flashlight up to the strip map of the route we'll be working on today. We've been doing this mission for over a month, so we pretty much have it down to a science. Nonetheless, outside the wire is outside the wire, and the enemy no doubt despises this mission.

The ground in Iraq is extremely hard. Not made for digging or planting; it's a landscaper's worst nightmare. IEDs work best when they're buried, so that convoys can't see them. But because of the hard earth, most IEDs are set on top of the ground.

As one goes off, it creates a small crater. As the insurgents set IEDs in the same craters over and over, the holes become bigger and bigger. Some of the holes are so big we can stand in them like we're inside a foxhole. The problem with craters this large is that convoys passing by them can't see the bombs until it's too late.

Our mission is to pour concrete into holes created by IEDs. Turks are helping us, and the insurgents hate this even more. American soldiers are one thing, but Muslim "traitors" are another. The Turks are the ones on post who mix and pour concrete for barriers, bunkers, landing pads, sidewalks, and buildings. They come out with us every day with two concrete mixing trucks.

We go outside the wire wearing full battle rattle. That's a full combat load, about fifty pounds. It's 125 degrees out, and we shovel debris out of the holes, pound rebar into the ground, rake the concrete even, and pull security.

In some spots whole sections of road are blown apart and degraded. A sister engineer company helps us with this. They use dozers, loaders, and graders to rip up the road, exposing the dirt underneath. This hard dirt becomes our canvas. We come in behind the sister company and pour a new concrete road.

We work in shifts. Ryan Ludwin is on the first team. I, the driver, am on the second. Tom Skavenski, the M60 gunner, is on the third. Ken Renninger, my A-driver, supervises. We take turns forming the concrete, manning the M60, and sitting in the Humvee cooling off in the heaven-sent air-conditioning system we've hooked up.

Two large tubes run from the trunk to the two front seats. They blow refreshing, cold air down the back of the necks of the driver and A-driver. We have a cooler with ice and water and we drink no less than four two-liter bottles of water every day.

When the two concrete mixers run out, two of the Humvees escort them back to the base for a refill, and everyone takes an MRE lunch. Afterward comes round two. We usually get back into base around three o'clock.

The schedule is never the same. For security, it can't be. Moving steadily down the road from nine to five on Monday through Friday would create a pattern. We work one day on/two days off, three days on/one day off, two days on/two days off. And we jump around the route like crack-addicted rabbits.

The hardest part of a lengthy mission like this is not becoming complacent. A month without attacks can really alter your perception of danger. That's just what the enemy wants. So we have to keep him guessing. We have to keep ourselves guessing. Every day we're out there the danger increases.

A medic from the sister engineer company nearly loses his foot on the mission. His Humvee moves off the road to the side of the job site. He finds a great spot to pull security. The enemy is counting on this great spot. By the time they see the IED sitting in the nearby bushes, it's too late. The medic is sent to Germany, where the doctors save his foot. The IED is small, and he is lucky.

Moments like this shatter us from our complacency. There are four vehicles, all Humvees. An all-Humvee convoy is a great way to travel because you can fly down the road without worrying about M916s or bulky concrete mixers having to keep up. The faster we go, the better the chances of throwing off the triggerman's timing.

We receive an additional mission outside of the route

we are working on. It's a giant IED crater on some side road. I am driving the third Humvee. Renninger is my A-driver, and Skavenski is our gunner. Ludwin, one of the concrete guys in third squad, doesn't come. Our small convoy drives to the recon site, and LT takes photos and notes. On the way back to camp LT, who's in the first Humvee, comes over the radio and says we're going to take a quick detour to the route we are currently working on. He just wants to check it out and find out whatever extra details he can.

We fly down the road, jumping on and off the large patches of concrete we poured. We spray-paint the pads, the canvas, while they are still wet. This is to ensure that after we leave and the concrete is still drying, no one can come and slip in an IED. We cruise over these random spray patterns.

Someone played tic-tac-toe on one part, and the Xs won. Someone else signed his name. I see THE 'SHROOM PLATOON, our self-proclaimed nickname. The 'Shroom Platoon because we're shit on all day and then left in the dark. It's a joke, but not really.

We travel sixty miles per hour down the unimproved road. The roar of the diesel engine is the only thing I can hear. I watch the vehicle ahead of me, the second one in the convoy. I continuously vary my distance, trying to throw off any timing a potential triggerman may have. The second

Humvee, call sign Hunter Two, swerves drastically to the left side of the road. On the right edge of the road, clear as day, there's a short black cylinder.

The adrenaline releases, and my mind focuses.

From the cylinder, across the hard tan earth, run two wires. One is black and the other is red.

We are too close to stop, and I slam the pedal to the floor.

The wires run for about a meter until they hit tall weeds that grow along an irrigation ditch. No one is around, but there's no way of knowing how far those wires run.

The handheld radio crackles to life.

"Did you see that, One?" the vehicle ahead of me asks LT.

Now we are almost on top of the small black cylinder. It's a land mine, and there's no time to stop.

"Get the fuck down, Ski!" Ken Renninger yells to our gunner.

If I stop now, we'll land somewhere directly before or directly after the IED, so I keep my foot to the floor and pray. I pull the Humvee as far to the left as I can, and we roar past the land mine.

That split second is an eternity. I anticipate the pop of point-blank thunder. I anticipate red pieces of Renninger flying into me. Think of zombies. There are three pictures hanging from the windshield. Two are school pictures of

Renninger's daughter and son. The other is of the Blessed Mary. She holds her son and a wide, sunburst halo shines from behind her head. The pictures swing to the right as I swerve the Humvee, bumper number H-105, to the left. Skavenski ducks inside the turret, the left side of his lip bulging with Copenhagen. Both my hands grip the wheel, and I teeter on the left edge of the road. The speedometer on the Humvee goes only to sixty. The needle is buried.

No pop.

One more vehicle, one more target, left in this convoy.

Arthur Dodds, who's a trucker back home, Pickleman's dad, is the A-driver. I struggle to see Hunter Four in my side mirror. I can't. The small armored window doesn't allow enough room for me to see the whole mirror. Renninger has his Kevlar pressed against his window. I wait for the popping of thunder.

"You past it yet, Four?" asks LT over the radio.

A couple seconds pass, an eternity, before Dodds responds.

"Yeah," the radio crackles.

"All Hunter elements, this is Hunter One," LT says. "Halt. Herringbone, over."

A herringbone is a staggered formation we use when stopping a convoy on the road. The first vehicle, which is always a gun truck, parks sideways across the middle of the road; its gunner faces twelve o'clock. The second vehicle, which doesn't have to be a gun truck but is today parks behind the first to the right side of the road; its gunner faces three o'clock. The third vehicle, which doesn't have to be a gun truck but is today parks behind the second vehicle to the left side of the road; its gunner faces nine o'clock. The last vehicle, which is always a gun truck, parks behind the third vehicle sideways across the middle of the road; its gunner faces six o'clock.

We immediately check the surroundings for a second set of IEDs. The enemy knows our tactics well enough to know that a four-Humvee convoy will usually blow past an IED and park a certain distance away. They'll sometimes set up a conspicuous IED like say, a land mine trailing with wires, and plant more inconspicuous explosives a certain distance away.

All is clear in our twenty-five meter sweep, and LT radios the EOD (Explosive Ordinance Disposal) team over the SINCGARS (Single Channel Ground and Airborne Radio System), the secure radio we use outside the wire to contact post command. Then he comes over the hand-held radio and gives us direction on where to go in order to secure the site. He knows this route like the back of his hand. He's sure that if we take a farming trail located off to our right and follow the irrigation ditch, it will come out on the road to a location well before the black land mine lying on the ground.

"Hunter Three, this is Hunter One, over," he says.

"One this is Three, over," Renninger responds.

"You follow me on this dirt trail to our right. Two and Four, secure this side. Nobody passes. Not even civilians. Over."

"Roger, One," Renninger says from our Humvee.

"Roger, One," says the A-driver of the second Humvee.

"Roger," says Dodds from the fourth Humvee.

Renninger lights a Marb Red and turns to Skavenski's legs. "Be ready, Ski."

"All right, Sarge," he says. Tom Skavenski is always ready.

We follow LT out and around the weed-enriched irrigation system. We try to drive fast here, but it's difficult on the bumpy dirt road. Nonetheless, we need to move as quickly as possible. Being on a paved road is one thing, but there's no telling what's hiding back here.

LT's Humvee throws up a cloud of dirt. The brown dirt has a brick red tint to it resembling rust. The tall weeds that outline the irrigation ditch whiz by. Their healthy green color also seems shadowed with rust. We follow the tall weeds. They remind me of a lengthy row of grapes in a vineyard. The dried clay thrown up by LT's Humvee now blocks my view. Skavenski chokes on the dust, and I have to back off.

"Still back there, Three?" LT asks over the radio.

"Yeah, we're here," says Renninger into the handheld, a puff of cigarette smoke blending with the dust in the air. "We'll follow your trail, over."

"Roger."

We pull around the first turn. A family of sustenance farmers stands off to the side. They're not used to seeing military convoys back here, and they give us a confused look. The children run to the edge and give us a thumbs-up. One of them motions for a bottle of water. We fly past them. There's no time for sentiment.

We get around the second corner and fly to the paved road. Once there we set up a small box formation. We pull sideways across the road so both drivers are facing toward the inside. Tom Skavenski points his turret toward six o'clock and Jason Demarco, LT's gunner, points his toward twelve o'clock.

We wait about thirty minutes, which is exceptionally short for this type of situation, until EOD shows up. They park in between our two box formations and break out the bomb-inspecting robot. They shortly conclude that the IED is a dud. It's a fake, conspicuous land mine and was set up only to watch our reaction.

The whole time there is a man standing three hundred meters away. He has a pair of binoculars and is watching our every move. We can't shoot him because of the Geneva convention. The Geneva convention is a series of agreements about the rules of war, and they say we can't shoot anyone who isn't holding a weapon and isn't posing an immediate threat to our convoy. Despite hours of self-debate we understand that it has to be this way.

Imagine if soldiers started shooting civilians without weapons in their hands. Imagine what the news media back home would do with our excuse: he was watching us with binoculars. Abu Ghraib prison torture would be a fairy tale by comparison.

This is how the enemy knows our tactics.

This is how we avoid remaining complacent.

We come back out for another month to paint our canvas with *haji* concrete and green spray paint. The days are long and hard, but the mission is important. It isn't immediately gratifying. We are sweaty and tired and the ripped-up road ahead of us seems much longer than the patched road behind us. Nonetheless, we are no doubt saving people's lives by accomplishing this mission. It's not direct, but if our efforts stop even one insurgent from reusing a crater to kill another soldier or civilian, the mission is worth it.

The local sheik even comes out to thank us when, with the help of the sister unit, we replace an irrigation pipe that ran under the road we were repairing. It had been broken for years. Even though we couldn't give the locals water when we flew past them after the fake IED, we provided them with irrigation water they hadn't seen in years.

This isn't a weapons cache-search mission during which we kick down doors looking for suspects. We pour concrete. No news reporters followed us around, because soldiers saving lives aren't as interesting as soldiers taking lives. America's not aware of the honor of war unless it involves POWs or medals of valor. Sometimes it's frustrating the way our efforts seem left on the ground in Iraq: spray paint on *haji* concrete.

The hard canvas we paint in Iraq is one of scar tissue. It's a bunch of holes crudely patched with cheap concrete. It's a stretch of road that was previously unmanageable. It's a makeshift job, but it works. It doesn't match the rest of the road, but The 'Shroom Platoon has done its part.

"What should we name him?" I ask.

"Jerkface," says Jesse Smith around the wad of Copenhagen that is packed behind his bottom lip.

"Let's see what kind of tricks he can do."

Jerkface is a small grayish brown bird. He is the color of rocks and dust, the color of Iraq. He is one of the several birds who live in the palm trees outside our barracks. Few birds are brave enough to come near us, but Jerkface often flies down for a visit.

Austin Rhodes and Justin Greene live in the lower-enlisted bay in which we built rooms before we moved in. And since we had control over the matter, they decided to combine their rooms to have a little extra space. They take Jerkface into their room where he sits on our hands like a trained parrot.

We play with the little bird, spread his legs apart, bob him up and down. We play "Rockin' Robin" from Greene's laptop and make Jerkface dance to it. We pass him from hand to hand, finger to finger, testing his patience.

We play with him like children play with stuffed animals. The whole time, he looks at us with dumb eyes. As he sits perched on my finger, dancing because I am making him, I study the content little bird. He is the size of any little robin or finch back home. He sits on my finger calm and collected, breathing casually, wondering about this new experience. I look at Jerkface and wonder if he knows how lucky he is to be dumb.

I think of looking at myself in the bathroom mirror at Fort Bragg. About nine months ago, as I was training for the Sandbox, I had the same dumb look on my face. I looked around at my new environment and wondered what it was all about. I took it all in, darted my head from side to side, and pecked at my food as some great, unseen force took me by the legs and forced me to dance.

Let's see what kind of tricks he can do.

In Iraq I sit in my barracks at night. On missions I lie on a cot or in the back of a Humvee. With each passing day I grow more desensitized and dumb. A mortar can come crashing through the barracks ceiling at any second. The side of the road can blow up anytime during a convoy— an RPG (Rocket Propelled Grenade) or AK-47 or friendly fire. But what's the point in worrying? So I sit calm and collected, breathing casually, wondering about this new experience.

When I want to eat, I go to the chow hall. Jerkface goes to the palm tree. When I want to play, I go to our makeshift volleyball court. Jerkface goes to the palm tree. When I want to talk to my family, I go to the Internet café. Jerkface goes to the palm tree.

I am occupying Jerkface's home, but he doesn't seem to mind. Maybe he thinks my Joe Schmo friends and I can make his home better. After all, we give him treats from the mountain of packages sitting on the shelf in the common room. Jerkface likes crackers. Even the ones from the MREs.

We eat MREs often enough to pity those soldiers who eat them every day. If you're wondering what it's like to eat an MRE in Iraq, try this:

First, disperse fifty pounds of gear between your head, shoulders, and chest. Then find your favorite piece of cardboard, smother it with cheese-flavored grease, and you have the pre-meal snack of cheese and crackers. For the MRE meal take another piece of cardboard and cut it into bite-sized pieces. Soak the cardboard pieces overnight in a mixture of coagulated gravy, Tabasco sauce, and old sticky tomatoes. Make sure you do this at room temperature. Preheat your oven to 140 degrees, but instead of cooking your meal, sit on the floor directly in front of the oven. Open the oven door, and place a fan inside so it blows in your face. Now tip your garbage can over to simulate any given Iraqi street and you have created the typical dining experience.

The kids in Iraq love MREs. Their eyes light up like Christmas candles when they see a box of MREs. They even know the acronym. They grab the bulging brown package out of our hands and sit criss-crossed with it in their lap. Ripping it open, they toss the spoon and utility pack full of napkins, salt, and matches over their shoulder. They always toss the spoon. They eat MREs with their hands, tearing into the "entrée" first, exposing the brown sludge that is supposed to pass for beefsteak and mushrooms. Not that it isn't beefsteak and mushrooms. It most certainly is. After all, turkey, cranberry sauce, croissants, and sweet potatoes are still a fine Thanksgiving meal even if they're pureed together and vacuum packed for three years, right?

When I think of elementary schoolkids in America peeling the crusts off their sandwiches, complaining that their parents won't buy them Lunchables, I pity them more than the Iraqi kids.

Even the dogs are weary of the MREs. Once, on the

IED crater-filling mission, a skinny little mutt comes up to us with a friendly grin. His hair is short and the color of Iraq, dusty red-brown. He flexes his nostrils at us as we spoon MRE slush into our mouths. We pet him on the head and name him Haji. He is a rather friendly pup, and we look for his collar. Yeah, right. There's a culturally based functional fixation if I ever saw one: expecting a wandering Iraqi dog to have proper identification.

My name is "Haji." I belong to Malhabar Azwiki at 666 North Ambush Drive, Balad, Iraq.

Haji the Dog looks like he hasn't eaten in weeks. He reminds me of those dogs they pick up on those animal cop shows, the ones that come from a 20x15 chain-link fenced backyard where twelve mangy mutts live in their own feces. We can see his ribs and feel his spine when we pet his back. But he looks happy and hopeful, like any other hungry dog.

Jesse Smith has ravioli, and he tosses a few pieces on the ground in front of Haji. He approaches the ravioli and gives it a sniff. I remember a little boy who tore into a similar MRE with such speed that he had no time for a spoon. Haji the Dog is starving. And he's a dog. Surely he'll swallow the ravioli without chewing and then beg us for more. He sniffs it once, pulls back, and sniffs it again. Then he turns and walks away. Haji seems insulted.

We throw our heads back in laughter. Haji the Dog trots

away, off to find some food worthy of his time and energy, and we finish our MREs. Maybe Haji is already too stuffed to enjoy the ravioli, but I doubt it.

There are two kinds of animals in war. There are the animals that live here. These animals, like Jerkface and Haji, give us perspective. They show us resilience and understanding. They show us reality, that we have no control over our situation. That MREs are disgusting.

But the other kind of animals in war, they break your heart. They're the animals you left back home. The ones you abandoned.

One night a letter lies on my bunk. The address on the front is in my father's handwriting: all capital letters that slant to the right. The handwriting from many of my childhood memories. Growing up, I looked up to that handwriting. It represented the man I was to become. I write in all capital letters now, too.

I love getting letters from my father. It is our own special time together, a time for regret, denial, and pride. My father is very articulate. He doesn't have a master's degree in English. He doesn't spit out six-syllable words in every sentence. But he has the truly rare ability to tell a story, to use language uniquely. Without conscious knowledge or intent, it's my dad who taught me to write.

I love reading his letters. I love hearing his stories.

I also admire my father's ability to chat. My father loves

talking to people, figuring them out, cluing in and finding out how innately similar we human beings are. My mother often says, "Your father would talk to a lamppost if he thought it would listen." My father has the gift of gab, and it has served him well. It even helps me while I sit on a slumped army bunk in the middle of Iraq wondering about tomorrow, if I should face a new mission with fear or faith.

Anticipating what new things he has to tell me, I sit holding his latest letter. It is in a thick envelope, and after opening it I see it comes with pictures: two digital pictures printed off a computer.

Dad tells me that the pictures are from Drake Island in Follensby Clear Pond, New York. My parents and a bunch of their friends camped out on a small state-owned island. They had bonfires and ate baked beans, hot dogs, and s'mores. They played cards and swam and swapped stories. All the real good stuff. The stuff fathers and sons do together to learn about each other.

Wish you could've been there, Ryan, he writes.

Me too, Dad.

The second half of the letter is about the hard reality of the trip, how afterward my parents put their dog, Haley, to sleep.

Haley had regained most of her control after being paralyzed, but her bowels never fully recovered. For two years she'd been crapping without control. She wore a doggy dia-per with a hole cut for the tail, but she hated it. My parents hated it, too. It wasn't fair to keep her alive like that.

I look at the two pictures. One is of all the guys gathered around a hand-built table made of logs. The table is cov-ered with liquor bottles. The men are smiling and bonding. Think of EQ platoon.

The other picture is of Haley and Dad. Haley sleeps underneath a collapsible chair, the kind that litters the side-walk during a Fourth of July fireworks show. My father sits in the chair above her. His shirt is off and a beer is in his hand: the Dad pose. He's wearing a bathing suit that is too high on his thighs—Dad shorts—and a cowboy hat rests in his lap.

We got to the boat launch, my dad writes (the boat launch is the only way to the island.) *I loaded the canoe with all my gear and tied Haley to the front seat. We headed into a ten mile-an-hour wind. She did okay until she saw a loon fifty feet away. She wanted to play, but tying her down worked well.*

All Haley ever wanted to do was play. Back half working or not, she wanted to chase sticks, my sister and me, the cat, Frisbees, or loons on a lake. On land she could hardly walk. If she got too excited over food or playtime, her back half collapsed and she dragged it behind her like a collaps-ible chair after the Fourth of July grand finale.

In the water, though, where she'd always been a natural, Haley was her old self. The rules of gravity were suspended and Haley pumped her back legs like she used to. She could play fetch again. She could run again. No weight on her legs. No pain. No puppy-dog-eye shame because she crapped on the kitchen floor again. Haley's mouth always formed a natural smile when she panted. Her smile in the water was ear to ear.

My father sits frozen in time in my hands. His best friend lies underneath his chair with her eyes closed and mouth in the dirt. Only my father knows it's her last outing.

My father has complete control over Haley's life. He has to play God, but he hates having to do so. He decides that she's had a good life. Her grand finale is the best it can possibly be. She swims just like she used to, plays like a puppy again, smiling from floppy ear to floppy ear.

I guess that's one good thing about dying young: you're remembered for your purity, vigor, and spontaneity. Dying young, you're remembered for your youth.

Still doesn't make it fair.

I took Haley to the vet in the morning . . .

Haley loved the vet. She loved the smell of other dogs. She loved to be social. She would bark at a lamppost if she thought it would listen.

. . . and buried her soon thereafter.

Something in that sentence reeks of regret. My father doesn't fully believe it was the best option. He hates having to play God.

She sat with me in the front seat on the way home.

Haley was never allowed in the front seat. She got too excited, too happy, and Dad yelled at her.

I cried like a baby the whole way back.

She is dead. My father's best friend is dead. I look at the picture again. Haley's grand finale. She looks happy and peaceful, collapsed there underneath the Fourth of July chair.

I put her in the grave with your "Who's your doggy?" bandanna still on her.

Heather and I had given Haley the bright blue bandanna. Haley loved it because we loved it.

I thought of all the good times I had with Haley. All the times I chased her in the snow or in a lake. All the times I tackled her and then she stood up ready for more. All the times I slept next to her on the floor. All her panting smiles. The way she used to lie on the floor, take a deep breath, and exhale deeply before her eyes closed.

I know now that when she was put to sleep, Haley didn't take a final, deep breath of air. She went to sleep out of her routine, because she didn't really go to sleep at all.

I laid her on her pad with all her stuffed animals around her.

The image sticks in my head as if I were there: Dad tossing Haley's toys, one by one into a shallow grave in the backyard: the squeaky bear with dried spit that caked its hair together, the yellow duck out of which she used to eat the stuffing, the stuffed hot dog with red ketchup and yellow mustard fabric sticking out of the top. And Haley . . .

She looked peaceful.

. . . wearing the faded blue bandanna we loved, she loved. Her distinguished white snout and golden fur. No pain. No puppy-dog-eye shame. She was finally resting. At peace.

Then I added another headstone to our pet cemetery.

Let's try and keep that a pet only *cemetery, Dad.*

Keep your head down over there, Ryan.

I wish it was that simple.

I miss you.

I miss you too, Dad.

I love you.

I love you too, Dad.

Slumped over my army bunk, I cry.

//////////// **BAZOONA CAT** ////////////

A group of kids surround us. Our convoy is stopped momentarily, and the dirt is flying through the air. Not a sandstorm, just the wind blowing dirt in the desert. As always the sun is out and I hold a semi-automatic rifle as I talk to the local kids. They are telling us about their lives. Their innocent lives.

"Farm," one says, pointing to the vast desert.

"You live on a farm over there?" I ask.

"Yes," he says. "There. We . . ." He makes a shoveling motion.

"Shovel?"

He shakes his head. He gets on his knees and pats the ground.

"You grow plants?"

"Yes."

"What types of plants?"

He shapes his hands into a ball about the size of a basketball.

"Water . . . ?" he says.

"Watermelon?"

"Yes!" he says, excited. "Watermelon! Very good, yes?"

"Yeah, I love watermelons."

The boy, his brothers, and his friends are so excited to hear this. We, the American GIs, might as well be from a different planet. The Iraqi kids look up to us in a way I can't describe. They understand how lucky we are to be from America. They understand better than we do. Still, they try to give us anything they have. It's appreciation. It's their culture.

"You want watermelon?"

"No." I laugh. "No, thank you."

"I run . . ." he says, pointing toward his farm. "I run. Get melon."

"No thanks. Maybe tomorrow," I offer. "Tomorrow . . . if we're here."

I know we won't be.

He nods his head with enthusiasm. I know he'll be standing here tomorrow holding a watermelon, probably a dozen watermelons. Our convoy isn't running this way tomorrow.

But he'll be standing there, waiting, holding watermelons for the Americans.

Another boy rushes to the front of the group. He has no shoes and he looks as if he's been learning the backstroke in a pile of dust. He wipes the sweat off his face with his dirty white robe and motions to his mouth.

"Water?" he asks.

I know he's been working in the fields all day. All of these kids have been. I remember being their age: nine or ten. Work was a distant concept, something moms and dads did to pay for drum lessons, cable television, and summer camp. These children work because their families can't survive without it.

They work because the top 5 percent of Iraq's population—those who have money, land, and power—don't have a reason to care about the other 95 percent.

I grab the kid a Gatorade from the cooler in our Humvee. It's dripping water, and just the feel of its cold plastic is a relief from the 120-degree sun.

The boy holds up the orange sports drink proudly, like a trophy, his smile wider than his face. His friends look at him as though he'd made the venture into manhood. They look at him like American boys look at the kid with the newest video game system.

Before the Americans came to Iraq Gatorade for these boys was unheard of, a dream, nonexistent. Water that tastes like flavored sugar? Juice that doesn't come from a fruit and made from water not pulled from the Tigris River? It was unreal and unobtainable.

This American Schmo pulls it from his Humvee like pocket lint. I hand out a half dozen Gatorades and water to the kids, who are trying to sneak peeks inside the Humvee.

One of them comes to me and holds out a small fuzzy object. It's white and appears homemade. He holds it up, showing it off.

"Can I see?" I ask.

He places it in my hand. It looks like a rabbit's foot but slightly modified. The top of its hide is pulled into two pointy ears and small beads are glued to the front for eyes. It even has pink stitching that makes a triangular nose. The baby soft, white fur extends from the bottom, creating a sort of fluffy dress.

It reminds me of the tissue-and-string ghosts I used to make in elementary school around Halloween. In an ugly sort of way, like a baby pug, it's remarkably cute. I can't tell if the little craft is designed to be a cat or an owl.

"Is it a cat?" I ask.

"Bazoona," the boy replies.

"Bazoona?"

"Yes."

"Does that mean cat?"

"Bazoona."

"Owl?"

"Bazoona."

"Like hooo-hooo." I mock an owl.

"Mreeow, mreeow," he says, and claws the air.

"A cat," I conclude.

"Bazoona," he corrects.

"Bazoona?"

"Yes."

"In English: cat."

"Cut," he repeats. I smile at him.

"Mreeow, mreeow," I say. "Cat."

"Cut."

"You got it."

"In Arabic: Bazoona," he says.

"Bazoona."

"Yes," he says, smiling. "You got it."

He gives me the Bazoona Cat in exchange for a Gatorade. The other kids admire their friend for learning some English from the American.

In all honesty, these kids shouldn't be this close to us and our Humvee. Our higher-ups would throw a hissy fit if they knew how we acted out on the road.

"Keep the kids away from you," the commander tells us at every briefing he attends. "The insurgents use them for attacks, and they are not to be trusted. And do not throw them water or MREs from your vehicles. I don't want any kids getting run over on one of my convoys."

We glare at him.

"I know. It breaks my heart, too." He tries to reason with us. "I want to give those kids as much water as I can spare. But that's not the SOP."

The thing about the commander is he doesn't convoy around with us enough to know what's going on in this war. He gets intelligence reports and memorandums, and as far as he's concerned, the words they contain are sacred. To him rules are rules, because that's his job.

But it's not ours. We GI Joe Schmos, we're used to breaking rules. We've seen the human side of this war. We've seen enough hate and ignorance in this country to look past memorandums and standard operating procedures. And we understand a thing or two about psychology.

These kids are the future of Iraq. They're the ones who'll decide whether or not this war means anything. Not the commander. Not American politicians or the press. It's the children who will always remember the Americans who stopped by their farm and handed out Gatorade. And they will remember that they weren't just Americans. They were American soldiers.

At the end of the day it's our job to make sure there are more kids who identify us as the soldiers who are generous as opposed to the soldiers who destroy villages. One day at a time, one child at a time, that's how we make a difference. That's the only way we can come out of this mess feeling like it's worth something.

Preserve the innocent. Protect those who deserve it most.

Sometimes I get out the fuzzy little rabbit foot. For a minute or two I sit smelling it, remembering the dirty farmland kids and the boy who taught me some Arabic. I taught him some English and we called it even.

//////////// **TEARS** ////////////

We convoy to Q-West one perfectly normal day. Bravo Company has its own convoy trailing behind us about forty-five minutes.

The thing that sucks about convoying for five straight hours is the padding in military vehicles might as well be plywood. And the small cabins packed full of basic necessities, coupled with the uncomfortable and heavy body armor, provide little room to shift weight. We try anyway but to no avail. Our asses go numb after the first hour.

And the second worst part is we drink gallons of water every day, not to mention Red Bull and coffee. So five hours with no pee breaks is impossible. We piss into empty bottles and toss them out of the truck.

But it's August. We're so used to this lifestyle we could do it in our sleep.

Upon arrival at Q-West we drive our convoy straight to the chow hall. There I see some of the Bravo guys who weren't on Bravo's convoy. Since February most of us have been rotated to Q-West. For a while we rotated a few guys up here every couple of weeks.

The first person I see is Juan Hernandez. He's an equipment operator, too, and we worked together back in February. Among other jobs, the biggest one was barricading the ECP (Entry Control Point) that serviced the camp.

An ECP is simply a gate where convoys or other personnel enter a high-security camp or FOB. Without fighting your way through the perimeter, there's no other way into a military post. Hernandez, I, and a few other soldiers from B company fortified the main ECP to the camp with Hesco barriers.

Hesco barriers look like 4x4x6-foot sandbags attached to each other, wrapped in wire mesh. They stand upright, tops open, and engineers use bucket loaders to fill them with dirt. The dirt to catch bullets.

"Hey, Hernandez!" I yell as I approach him in the chow hall's gravel parking lot.

"Hey, Smithson," he said. "How are you?"

"Same shit, different day. You?"

"I'm all right."

Hernandez seems distant, but this happens when you're in a combat zone. A lot of us feel distant. Distant from family. Distant from love. Distant from life.

So I don't think anything of it.

After getting our meals we sit down with a group of Bravo guys.

"Hey, Smithson," says Sergeant Stone. "Good to see you. How've you been?"

"Good, Sarge," I say. "Starving."

As I eat, I notice the whole group seems distant.

"You guys all right?" I ask them.

"You didn't hear?" says Hernandez.

I shake my head.

"Sergeant Conklin died today," he says. "He was on the convoy behind you."

"Oh, man," I say. "IED?"

Hernandez nods his head.

Ten months into this tour we haven't lost anyone, and now, out of nowhere . . .

"Was he the one who worked out a lot?"

"Yeah, he was on that ECP mission with us."

"And he was a sergeant?" I say.

I try to picture the sergeants of B company, those with whom I worked back in February. "The only sergeants I remember out on the ECP are Stone and that crazy old guy, what is his name?"

"Blake."

"Yeah, Blake," I say.

I had almost forgotten. Blake was a fanatical old man. Picture Christopher Lloyd wearing a desert Kevlar. Picture him laughing with an unfiltered cigarette in his mouth and jabbing at your ribs. His eyes are decorated with crow's feet, and his unbuttoned chin strap swings around as he laughs.

I want to share the memory. I want to tell Juan Hernandez all about it and laugh with him, but the painful look on his face stops me.

"I think he made sergeant after you left," says Stone. "You'd know him as a specialist."

"Yeah, yeah. I remember him," I lie.

I remember that Jim Conklin worked out a lot, but I don't remember Jim Conklin. He is these guys' brother, he died forty-five minutes behind me, and I am ashamed that I can't recall a single moment with him.

We sit in silence for a while reflecting, eating, wondering about life and war and peace and death.

"You guys okay?" I ask Jim Conklin's brothers. They shrug. Really because they don't know. Reality hasn't set in yet. It's even too early for shock.

Then Stone says, "People die."

He shoves a piece of army steak into his mouth and chews.

I am shocked at the insensitivity. I try to place myself in their shoes. I picture losing someone like Sebastian Koprowski or Todd Wegner, Scott Moore or Jesse Smith, Josh Roman or . . . anyone. I almost cry at the mere thought. And this guy shrugs it off with "People die"?

I mean, for Christ's sake, show some emotion. Your fellow soldier was just bombed to death. *Our* fellow soldier. And some ignorant *haji* flipped the trigger. What happened to vengeance and spitefulness? What happened to hate? What happened to winning the war?

Then it hits me: Showing emotion shows vulnerability, and vulnerability gives into the fear. It's not a macho thing. It's about the need to survive. That's what terrorism is all about: mortal fear. If we let the fear take over, we lose. We can't lose. We have to stay strong. There's a time and place for grieving, and it's not in the chow hall eating boot leather covered in A.1. steak sauce.

People die.

Insensitive. True.

This is a war. We forget that sometimes. A hundred successful convoys and you tend to forget. Before I left the States a thousand and one people told me to avoid getting complacent, especially those who served in Vietnam. We never really become complacent. Our eyes are always open, always ready, but sometimes we do forget that we're in a combat zone.

B company lives in old airplane hangars. Cots and wall lockers are scattered across the hangar's concrete floor. Some have towels or ponchos strung up with 550 cord to provide privacy. Some have stuffed animals from girlfriends and wives. Some have TVs. Some have laptops. Some have pictures and birthday cards and nonperishable food.

And everything is needlessly camouflaged. The army-issue brown towels, the army green cots and socks and ponchos, the tan wall lockers and desert boots and desert uniforms. The place is decorated in the classic style that is the army. It's ugly. It's beautiful.

Hernandez points to a locker that looks like all the rest and says, "That's his."

I can't remember who Conklin is. I can't put a face to the name, so Hernandez shows me. Conklin's tan wall locker is covered with pictures. Most are of his family. Some are of him and his B company friends. I study the pictures carefully, trying to hear his voice in my head, trying to remember a conversation we had.

In his pictures Jim Conklin is young and full of life. He smiles in every one. Pictures of soldiers in a combat zone rarely have people smiling. But Jim seemed to be a genuinely happy person, and now I remember what he looked like. But there's still a problem. I can't remember *who* he was.

Conklin's bed is made. It's a cot with a sleeping bag on top, so maybe "made" is an overstatement. His bed is neat. The brown T-shirt he used as a pillowcase is covered in drool stains. Some of his friends have placed his rosary neatly on his army brown pillow. Conklin was a devout Catholic.

One of his friends, the guy on the cot next to him, takes a break from a PlayStation game. The screen is temporarily frozen, and the level is loading. He looks down toward the neatly displayed rosary and stares. He stares at Jim Conklin's empty cot.

What is he thinking about?

He's remembering the smell of Conklin's aftershave, the sound of Conklin's voice, maybe a conversation they had. A philosophical conversation about life and death because that's how soldiers sometimes talk to each other.

He doesn't cry; he doesn't even really look sad. He looks thoughtful. He just stares, in an unguarded moment, as if nothing else in the world matters. Not the hangar, not the video game, not the heat, not the war, not anything.

He's wondering where Jim Conklin is now, how he can just be . . . gone. He's wondering what Jim's parents are like and how his mom will carry on after she gets the news. He's wondering how *his* mom would carry on if she heard similar news. He's wondering why it hurts so much.

He learns things while staring at his dead friend's empty cot. He learns that life is not everything he thought it was.

He learns what war means. He learns what peace means. He learns that death is nondiscriminatory. He learns that after ten solid months, James H. Conklin will not walk through the hangar door later tonight. He will not stow his gear and share a meaningful conversation while he unlaces his boots. He will not rub foot powder into his cracked feet, read a chapter in a book, and then drool on the brown T-shirt he used as a pillowcase.

Not tonight, not ever again.

A week later, we make another LOGPAC up to Q-West. For supplies, sure. But mostly we go for Jim Conklin's funeral. A hundred people sit in fold-out chairs.

They start with a slideshow full of pictures of Conklin. It's to the song "Forever Young." Jim Conklin was twenty-two when he was blown up. "Forever Young," indeed. A piece of shrapnel from an IED is what did him in. It was on August 21, nine days before my birthday, fifteen after his. Jim hardly knew what hit him. He died of shock, says the medic from B company.

I say he died from joining the army.

A guy who was twenty-two, liked by everyone, smart, athletic, funny, charming, hard working, and whose voice I can't hear in my head, has died. And I was on the road forty-five minutes ahead of him, pissing into a bottle when he was killed.

Here I am at a man's funeral and I hardly knew him. Why didn't I get to know him better? What the hell is wrong with me? Maybe I should have seen it coming. How could I have seen this coming? Ten months into the tour and we haven't lost a single person. Then we lose Jim Conklin.

I sit in my fold-out chair. One of Conklin's buddies goes onstage. He has a guitar, and another guy holds up a microphone so we can all hear the words to the song he wrote. The guy singing, he's holding back tears because he's not vulnerable.

It dawns on me that Conklin died five days ago. This guy wrote this song in less than a week. That's pretty impressive, and I respect it. It doesn't draw tears, really. It's not that good. But it's a song about a fallen soldier. It's exceptional.

He leaves and a couple soldiers who were closest to Conklin say a few words. But I don't know them. I know their names; throughout the tour, I've worked with all of them, but I don't know them. They know Jim Conklin like a brother. Their speeches draw tears.

But I don't cry. The crowd is sniffling, but I hold mine back. Vulnerability, sure. Detachment, sure. But it's more than that.

I hardly knew Jim Conklin. I worked with him, yes, for two weeks in February, but I don't really remember him. I am ashamed, and this is why I hold back tears. I feel like crying, but I feel like it's not my place to cry.

Jim Conklin's real friends have gone through hell since he died. This hell will always be a part of them, and I don't share that. I'm not entitled to share tears. I told my friends from Bravo company, I told Jim Conklin, that I'd come back.

"It was great to work with you," I said. "I'll be back soon."

They truly are an exceptional group of people. I told them I'd volunteer to come back for another rotation at Q-West, but I never did. There were a lot of other missions going on, and I got lost in the mess. I could've told Renninger to send me back, but I didn't. I betrayed them. I betrayed Jim. Now he is dead, and I'm not entitled to tears.

His best friend is done talking, and the whole room sniffles.

I stare at the M16 up onstage. Jim Conklin's rifle, upside down and wearing his Kevlar and dog tags, standing alone onstage. A small box sits beside it on the ground. It has a clear face, and inside, arranged neatly, are all of his medals and awards. An eleven by fourteen framed portrait of Conklin in his dress greens sits on a stand.

Bravo company's first sergeant, the enlisted soldier who works directly with the commander, takes the stand and does what's called the "Last Call."

"Staff Sergeant Holmes," he says, reading the names off a paper.

Somewhere in the crowd: "Here, First Sergeant."

"Specialist Carlton."

"Here, First Sergeant."

"Sergeant First Class Blake."

"Here, First Sergeant."

"Sergeant Conklin."

And the whole room is silent.

"Sergeant Jim Conklin," the First Sergeant says again.

No one says a word.

"Sergeant James Henry Conklin."

Nothing.

And then he tells us to stand for the twenty-one-gun salute. Seven people stand at attention off to the left. Someone standing beside them gives orders, and they each fire three synchronized, blank rounds at the ceiling.

Jim Conklin did not die in my arms. I didn't witness his death. I didn't call in the "nine line" report to have him medevaced out of the kill zone. I didn't know him. I forgot who he was, and I can't hear his voice in my head. I told him I'd volunteer for another rotation and I didn't. Maybe I would remember him better if I'd come up a second or third time, but I didn't.

We stay standing while someone plays taps.

The first set of three notes is played. They're slow,

precise, and perfect. My bottom lip quivers, but I am not entitled to tears.

The second set of three notes is played. My eyes water, and the room turns blurry.

I didn't know him, this true GI Joe Schmo, this hero. He is not my family or close friend. I cannot picture a moment of interaction between the two of us. I know who he is, but I don't know him. His existence meant nothing to me. And at this moment his existence means everything to me.

Picture a fence in New York City. Picture being stuck in it.

My eyes are blurry, and I choke on my own tears. I feel as if I'm trapped in rubble, and the weight of James H. Conklin's last good-bye is overwhelming.

I shed tears I don't deserve to shed. I'm not entitled to tears, but they come nonetheless. They are not quiet, respectful, funeral tears. They are tears for a fellow soldier, a brother I hardly knew, and I sob like a baby. I bury my face in my hands like a mother who puts flowers by her dead son's picture, like Jim Conklin's mother.

I have lost nothing in Jim Conklin's death, but in a way I have lost everything.

These tears for injustice, for impurity, for virtue, for love, for hate, for misunderstanding, for innocence, for guilt, for nothing, and for everything.

PART III
/////////// BLUE PHASE ////////////

/// BASIC TRAINING PART III ///

nly after we have been completely destroyed can we begin to find ourselves.

The drill sergeants do it like this: they break us down, build us up, break us down again, and then build us back up. The first breakdown is the hardest part. It's the first three weeks, and they call it Red Phase. The second three weeks is called White Phase. And this is when they build us up.

The third three weeks, that's Blue Phase. It's nearing the end, but there's always one more trick up their sleeve, one more breakdown before we can be built into soldiers.

During the second to last week of blue phase there's an FTX. The first field training exercise we'll ever conduct in the military. The whole company camps out in the Missouri woods. It's December, and we pull security shifts at all hours of the night. There's a select group of privates called OPFOR (Opposing Force) who try to enter our perimeter. So we have to be aware.

The whole time we wear laser gear: a bunch of sensors attached to our chests, shoulders, and helmet. If they get hit by an opponent's laser, they chirp loudly until a drill sergeant finds us and sticks a yellow key into the box on our chests.

There's another box on the end of our weapon. This is how we shoot a laser. The way it works is off of blank rounds: simply gunpowder without a bullet. And the way M16s work is with direct impingement. This means that there's a tube in the barrel to collect the high pressure gas expelled from a detonated round. The gas is then used to push the hammer back down, thus recharging the weapon. What you get from direct impingement is semiautomatic gunfire.

The box sitting on the muzzle of our M16 needs some of that expelled gas in order to fire. When the trigger is pulled, the box shoots a laser wherever the rifle is aimed. And since it can work only when a blank round actually goes off, this army laser gear is about as real as it gets.

Within the platoon we pair off in battle buddy teams. Each battle buddy watches the other's back. Each battle buddy team sleeps in two-person tents called pup tents. And our pup tents line the edge of the section of perimeter for which fourth platoon is responsible. The only other tents on the FTX are a warming tent and a chow tent.

Upon arrival at the site we dig "haste" fighting positions using our E-tools. A haste is a little burrow in the ground, just a spot to lie down and be concealed from the enemy. Then we plant sticks in the ground to mark our "sectors of fire." At the forefront of my haste, facing outside the perimeter, there's one stick on the left and one on the right. Picture a 7-10 split in bowling. Picture a rifle between the two pins. The pins, or sticks, keep me from firing too far left or right. This way, we don't shoot into each other's sectors and possibly each other's positions.

My battle buddy and I, we're smart. We find leaves and fill our hastes with them. Then we lay our ponchos on top of the leaves. See, air is an insulator, and a pile of leaves has a lot of air in it. During the FTX we'll have to lie for hours in our hastes. So a pile of leaves protects us from the frozen December ground. After all, that's how we'd do it in war.

Also like in a real combat zone, we don't just sleep in tents and pull security shifts. A large part of the FTX is running missions.

"B team, bounce forward!" I yell. I am the B team leader for this mission. Our five-man group jumps up from their prone positions and hauls ass for five seconds.

I'm up. . . . You see me. . . . I'm down.

Fifteen meters from where we started, we all drop to our knees to our hands to our stomachs. All of this at the same time, dress, right, dressed, and no less than ten meters apart. Ten meters is the proper distancing between soldiers.

In my head the drill sergeant corrects me. *There are no soldiers here. Only lousy privates.*

Ten meters because that's the effective range of a grenade. If we're too close together when a grenade falls, the private next to me gets wasted, too.

So we're ten meters apart from each other, and a sniper is taking shots from the other side of the valley. He's already taken out one guy from A team, who fight from the other side of the shallow ravine. They're closer to the sniper than we are.

But I see him, that sniper, that single OPFOR guy crouching, taking shots at us. He's just another private from basic training, but right now he's the enemy.

There's a log lying a little ways ahead of me. I can get to it. I can use it for protection. I crawl on my stomach just like we did across The Pit, my belly dragging on the ground, my muzzle out of the dirt and leaves.

I get behind the log. Safe. The other four members of my team are lying on their stomachs, ready for the chance to take this guy out. I see him pointing his weapon at them. I make my move.

I crouch behind the log and take a kneeling position.

He sees me.

I point my weapon at him. He points his at me.

BRASS. It stands for Breathe, Relax, Aim, Sight picture, Squeeze. And it's the only army acronym that matters right now.

Breathe.

Breathe methodically. Time the breaths. Figure them out. This is harder than it sounds. Ever consciously think about blinking? Drives you crazy trying to control it. You can hardly tell when it needs to be done. Too much? Too little? Too automatic. There's a natural pause at the end of an exhale. That's when you shoot.

Relax.

Muscles fatigue quickly in one position. Rest the back of the elbow on the knee. A pointy elbow can't balance on the point of a knee without wiggling around. And more important, pull the weapon into the shoulder. Don't try to hold it in the air. Pulling the weapon snug is easier than trying to fight gravity. Fight gravity and you'll lose every time.

Aim.

Aim low. Keep the sides of the front sight post flush with his body. Bullets arch like baseballs. The round will climb for the first hundred or so meters. Put the front sight post where the target meets the dirt. Even if the bullet skims the ground in front of him, it'll bounce upward.

Sight picture.

Put the front sight post in the middle of the rear aperture. The black circular opening of the rear aperture is fuzzy, because the focus is on the target. Then it's on the front sight post. When they're lined up, move the back of the weapon so the front sight post sits in the center of the fuzzy hole. Smack dab in the center.

Squeeze.

Don't pull the trigger. If the penny falls, it's ten push-ups. Squeeze, control the trigger, and feel the hammer fall. The hammer should surprise you every time. Shouldn't know it's coming. Neither should the bad guy.

BANG

The hammer should surprise me. It does. But not my hammer.

His hammer.

The bad guy, OPFOR, has a better shot, a faster shot than me. I am hit, and B team has no leader. There's a loud chirping noise to remind me.

"Fall down," says the drill sergeant, sticking a yellow key into my chest. "You're dead."

My laser gear stops chirping, and I lie in the leaves. I shouldn't have kneeled. I was fine behind the log. I was safe. I should have stayed in the prone and aimed over the log. I exposed too much by kneeling.

The drill sergeant looks at me, pulls out a CS gas grenade, tear gas, and winks as he pulls the pin.

"Your team is screwed, private," he tells me.

He throws the canister next to the private who's taken over my command. The private rolls to his right, yells "Gas! Gas! Gas!" to his teammates, and undoes the protective mask carrier on his hip. He tries with shaky hands to get the mask on before the gas hits him. He's coughing as he puts it on.

"You're dead," the drill sergeant tells him.

I put my mask on. Then I sigh. I watch the losing battle continue like a spirit would after leaving its body.

Another one of us gets shot. And another.

Laser gear chirping all over the place. It fills the once-quiet woods.

"You're all dead," says the drill sergeant. He cuts the exercise short. "Friggin' embarrassment."

He keys the rest of the dead privates and the chirping stops. The Missouri woods go quiet again, and he rallies us together for an AAR (After Action Review). We sit in a semicircle facing him. These Missouri leaves we sit in, they're not orange and yellow like New York leaves. They're ugly and brown. The trees look down on us. Our whole squad was taken out by one guy. One guy and a "mustard gas" mortar round.

The drill sergeant kicks the CS canister toward the edge of the woods, and the OPFOR member who was shooting at us runs the other way, getting ready for another bunch of privates to come strolling through. Getting ready to show them just how underprepared for war they are.

The drill sergeant asks us what went wrong. We sit in silence because we have no idea. The execution of war looks so easy in the movies. The reality of war, though, is much more complicated.

If this were real I'd be dead, I think.

I wasn't even taken out by a soldier. It was one of the privates of my basic training company. Some GI Joe Schmo who's not even a GI yet. The gas expelled from his blank round set a laser shooting from the OD green box on the end of his rifle. The blank ejected into the Missouri leaves, and the laser raced across the small valley toward me: the target. The laser landed in one of the receptors on my chest, helmet, or shoulders. And he killed me before I had a chance to shoot.

We're playing laser tag with blank rounds and cool army gear. If someone had told me this when I was six, I would have looked at them in marvel, wondering how I could possibly be so cool. I would have seen my future self as a hero. I would have thought of myself as one of those valiant, stone-jawed warriors in World War II and Vietnam flicks. Maybe Matt Damon or Mel Gibson.

Maybe Willem Dafoe or Charlie Sheen.

"What went wrong?" the drill sergeant asks me.

"I got shot, Drill Sergeant," I say.

"No shit, Einstein," he says. "But why?"

"I kneeled."

"That wasn't the problem," he says. "You shouldn't have bounced forward."

"It was only one guy."

"You should have bounced back, private," he says. "You didn't know if there were fifty guys lined up around the next curve. Your soldiers' lives were more important than the mission."

I forgot all about the original mission. We weren't supposed to be looking for and killing OPFOR. We were supposed to locate a nearby road. We were supposed to be doing reconnaissance so the army could move tanks. But finding the road was not important enough to die for.

I got caught up in winning *(The bad guys always lose)*. I got caught up in destroying him *(gooks in Vietnam flicks)*, in being a soldier *(No soldiers here, only lousy privates)*. I shouldn't have bounced forward *(Didn't I see that in a movie once?)*. I got caught up in avenging 9/11 *(That's why I'm here)*, in being . . .

"A hero," says the drill sergeant. "You were trying to be a hero."

"Yes, Drill Sergeant," I say.

Think of the FTX as a breakdown: the final test before we can become soldiers.

In Red Phase we're screamed at, told we're worthless. We learn hand-to-hand combat and marching basics. We learn how to eat a full meal in three minutes and how to ignore the stresses of having no self-expression. The lesson, really, is freedom.

In White Phase we learn how to shoot an M16 and how to work as a team. We learn how to work under pressure and strive toward a goal. We learn to believe in ourselves and our abilities. The lesson, really, is faith.

In Blue Phase we learn that no one is ever prepared for war. We learn that no matter how many drills you run or how many push-ups you do, you're never good enough. There's always someone better; there's always another trick up a sleeve. The lesson, really, is humility.

And then we graduate. We walk tall across the stage but not too tall. Our families come down to watch us, to say they're proud. Us in our Class A uniforms, amazed at the nine-week journey we've taken. Proud of our accomplishment but not too proud. The best part is not when our families congratulate us or when we walk across the stage. The best part is after the ceremony when the drill sergeant shakes our hands.

"Congratulations, soldier," he says.

I stay at Fort Leonard Wood for AIT where, for nine

more weeks, I learn how to run heavy equipment. In March when I graduate, I finally return home to my family.

After they graduate basic training new soldiers have an opportunity to do what's called "hometown recruiting." About 99 percent of all basic training grads are highly motivated to be a part of the American defense system. And hometown recruiting is the army's chance to let these soldiers flaunt their spirit in hopes it will catch others in its wake.

Plus, it's a couple more weeks of active duty pay, and since I have nothing better to do, I figure why not?

The recruiter with whom I work is a ranger. He's a sergeant first class, and he is authorized to wear four different combat patches. He has been shot twice, once in each leg, and quite literally fits every stereotype associated with the American soldier.

His uniform is decorated with medals I didn't even know existed. His exterior, the way he carries himself, is hard and unforgiving. In fact, upon receiving his request for drill sergeant school, the army decided he'd make a better recruiter because, my hand to God, he "is too mean."

Despite how the army labels him, I find the ranger to be one of the most interesting and insightful people I've ever met.

"I'll tell you what, Smithson," he says as he drives us to a local high school. "I would much rather be a drill sergeant. I hate this recruiting shit."

"This doesn't seem so bad, Sergeant," I say.

He shakes his head.

"These kids at these high schools," he says. "These kids for whom you gave up your future and put on that uniform, they don't even deserve it. They hardly respect you. They think you're some brainwashed grunt who has nothing better to do than join the army."

"They're just kids," I say. "They can't understand—"

"*You're* just a kid, Smithson," he says. "You don't understand what war is, do you?"

"No, Sergeant."

"But you understand your freedom."

"Yes."

"And that's what separates them from you," he says. "They take their freedom for granted because it's always been there."

"Yeah, but going through basic is what made me understand."

"You new recruits. You need to stop telling yourself that," he says. "You can't understand freedom until you give it up. And that's just what you did down at the MEPS station, isn't it?"

"I guess so."

"No, it's not a guessing game," he says. "Before you ever

set foot in basic training, you voluntarily gave up your freedom at the MEPS station."

"Yeah."

"And that was in high school, right?"

"Yes."

"How many other kids in your class joined the military?"

"A few."

"Exactly," he says. "These kids we're going to try to recruit today, they think recruiters lie and cheat and trick kids into joining. You just watch. Most of them won't even look at us. And they think they've got it all figured out. They think they know what democracy is because they study it in history class. They think they know what a dictatorship means because they read the definition in a book.

"But they don't have a clue, Smithson. Because if they did, they'd look you straight in the eye and thank you for what you're doing."

"Then what is a dictatorship, Sergeant?" I say.

"You want to know what a dictatorship is?"

"Yeah, why are we trying to overthrow the government in Iraq just because we don't agree with it?"

"You kids," he says, shaking his head. "You think everything is about ideals and proving points. Iraq is about human suffering. War, it's about human suffering."

He doesn't say anything for a few moments. He stares ahead, the highway passing us on all sides. Finally, he takes a breath and tells me a story.

"It was during the first Gulf War," he says.

Desert Storm in '91. He was a kid like me, fresh out of ranger school and living in Iraq. The public didn't even know about the mission he was running. To this day he can't discuss details. But he can tell me that he witnessed some soldiers from the Iraqi army trying to take a boy away from his mother.

The Iraqi army at that time was run by Saddam Hussein, the dictator of Iraq.

It took place on the outskirts of a little village. They lived in a little mud hut, just the boy and his mother. They were sustenance farmers. The mother's face was covered with a black cloth, as was required by law.

The boy's face was dirty since he hadn't yet rinsed off in the nearby irrigation ditch. He was pulled by his arm away from his mother. The Iraqi army, this was how they did their recruiting.

The soldiers threw the boy in the back of a pickup truck. The mother begged the soldiers to let her son go.

"He's only twelve years old!" she screamed in Arabic. "I need him on the farm!"

Howling in sorrow, the mother ran after her child. The boy sat in the pickup truck, helpless, being held by his arm.

One of the soldiers turned and shot the woman, point-blank, in the face. Her body fell limp to the ground, her face dismembered. The son watched it all happen, watched his mother die in a pool of her own blood. The truck took off, and the boy began his service in the Iraqi army.

"We couldn't reveal our position," says the recruiter. "We had to sit there in the irrigation ditch and watch it all happen, just like that little boy."

I think of the students at the school to which we're going. I think of their designer jeans and backward hats and iPod earphones. I think of them sitting at cafeteria tables in a high school paid for by the government, by their parents' tax money. I think of how they complain about their mother's brown sack lunches. How they complain that they didn't get enough for Christmas.

And then I think of that little boy, pulled by his arm away from the only person he had: his mother.

We pull up to the school; some kids who are probably sneaking cigarettes look away and put their hands in their pockets. With their backs facing us they walk toward the main entrance.

The recruiter shuts the car off and looks me straight in the eye.

"Let me ask you something," he says. "And be honest."

"Okay."

"Do you appreciate your freedom?"

"Yes, of course."

"Do you appreciate your freedom so much that you're willing to fight for it?"

"Yes."

"Okay," he says. "Do you appreciate your freedom so much that you're willing to fight for the freedom of others?"

I think for a moment, really trying to answer this question honestly.

"Yeah, I think so," I say. "Yes."

"That, Smithson," he says, "is why you deserve to wear this uniform. And I'm telling you right now, if that's really the way you feel, then the army needs more soldiers like you in Iraq."

"Why?" I ask.

"Those people deserve to be free," he says.

He's looking me straight in the eye, but his eyes are not even in the vehicle.

Dear Heather,

Hey, babe, how are you? Hope everything is going well back home. We don't have a date to come home yet, but it's coming. God, I can't wait. . . .

But guess what! I think I just had the best day so far since I've been stuck in this damn place. It doesn't really make up for the two hundred bad days, but it's something! I guess I'll start from the top.

My first task of the day was to go finish a job I was working on yesterday with a scoop loader. Yesterday I took the green military loader, because our Caterpillar loader was being serviced by the CAT guys. Today the CAT was finished, and I got to take it out. What a relief.

See, the difference between military equipment and civilian equipment is that civilian equipment is designed with the operator in mind. Most military junk is built so it kind of runs okay, and then a sort of chair is just fastened on top of it all. The CAT is so smooth to operate, as opposed to the cruel ragdoll tossing that goes on in the green loader. Plus, the CAT is air-conditioned so I don't have to perspire in places that haven't been wet since childbirth. Sorry, that was gross.

After my morning task I went to the really good chow hall for lunch. It's on the air force side of camp and has just started using real plates and silverware. Since I usually walk to chow, I eat at the closer one, which uses plastic plates and forks. Our squad leader loaned a bunch of us a Humvee and we drove across base to feel human again. I ate with forks that don't break when they try to stab carrots and off plates that don't have compartments.

It's really odd what the army makes you appreciate: hot showers, dry feet, plates....

In the afternoon I finished up a project we were also working on yesterday. We had to unload tents and tent poles from a storage container. After taking them out, we loaded them on pallets and then loaded the pallets onto three tractor trailers. There were a lot of tents and it was 115 degrees out, so that wasn't great.

But, get this, the reason we were loading them was to give them away to another unit. We no longer need them, and we were lightening our load for when we come home. Yes, I said HOME! There is a light at the end of the tunnel, and I saw it today. We are starting to conduct inventories and other stuff that will eventually lead to our departure from this place. It's pretty exciting!

After the tents there were cots that also had to be tossed. While we were behind our barracks loading the cots, the shower guy came over. I think I've told you about him, but I'll clarify anyway. He's the civilian who lives in a tent behind our shower and bathroom trailers and gets paid to keep them clean. He does an excellent job, and he's very nice. I try to talk to him sometimes, but he is from India and doesn't speak English very well. Nonetheless, he's extremely friendly, and we all appreciate the work he does for us.

Anyway, he came over and asked us to "make table" as he pointed to a stack of plywood lying on the ground. Carrion and I asked the supply sergeant for tools and we started building. We came to find out that he meant shelf rather than table, and after a very long, confusing discussion about dimensions and whatnot (damn language barriers) we got it built. It had sides, a back, and three shelves, and it fit perfectly in a little nook in his tent. He was very appreciative and thanked us a number of times. We figured it was the least we could do for what he does for us.

After we brought the shower guy his shelf we were off duty, and I walked to the gym. I had a good workout, and I followed it up with a great dinner at the closest chow hall. I was by myself, since my usual workout partner is on a mission for a few days, so I sat at the end of an empty table.

A civilian came and sat across from me. He spoke very good English, and I came to discover that he works as a translator for the military. I've tried talking to a handful of Iraqi civilians, but most are pretty limited in their English skills. It's usually hard to have an in-depth conversation with them. I decided that this was a rare chance, so I took it. I asked the translator if he thought Iraq was better now than it was a few years ago.

"The insurgents are getting worse, but the government, our freedoms, and way of life are much better," he said. "Five years ago if I said 'I don't like Saddam,' I would have been killed."

He said that now the people of Iraq have the freedom to do and say as they wish without fear, and that most are very grateful. He said the ones who don't like the changes are those in the cities like Tikrit, Mosul, Baghdad, Samarra, Fallujah. (You know, the cities always in the news.) But the people in the little villages love our efforts. That explains why it feels like we're in a parade when we convoy!

I asked him why there was such a difference in opinion.

"The people in the cities had money and power before the U.S. came here," he said. "They didn't need your help."

He also pointed out that most of the country is made up

of small villages and towns. A small minority hold the entire country's power, and it is they who oppose our cause.

He mentioned that insurgents attacked a water tower with rockets a few days ago. I asked him why they would do that since it doesn't hurt anyone but the locals who use the tower.

"Because they're crazy," he said. "There were no Americans to kill, so they attacked their own people. They have to destroy something."

We talked a little more about what I do, and I finished my meal. I got up and he offered his hand. I shook it, and he thanked me for talking to him and for helping his country.

Just thought I'd share that with you. I'll send an e-mail to everyone, too, but I'm pretty tired right now. So good night, babe.

Love You, Miss You,

Ryan

############## **IRONY** ///////////////////

The soldiers from our replacement unit are staying in Tent City, the same tents where we stayed upon our arrival back in December. It's now November. With the exception of a few guys on their second tour the replacements are brand-new to the war. And it's our job to show them the ropes.

It's the last mission I conduct in Iraq. I am driving the last gun truck in a convoy of eleven vehicles. SSG Robert Gasparotto is my A-driver, and our gunner is Zerega. There are two guys from the replacement unit in the back-seats among gear, water, and ammo cans.

They didn't convoy into Iraq like we did because they didn't bring any of their own equipment. Our unit is handing all of our equipment over to them, which for us, is a good thing. This means when we fly back to Fort Bragg, we won't have to stay and get all the equipment off the navy ships. We can simply out-process and go home.

But right now we sit at the gate of Anaconda waiting to go on our last mission. I look back at the new guys. One is a bit older than the other, and he looks a little more calm. The other one, the kid, looks scared shitless.

"So you guys just drive through an attack?" he asks.

"Yep," I say. "There's not much else to do."

After a while in a combat zone you start to think of everything as fateful. Something blows up, and it's fate. Get lucky when an IED is a dud, that's fate, too. Jim Conklin dies while on a simple LOGPAC mission, you guessed it: fate. And if today's the day, this last mission, well, then fuck it. At least we know God enjoys some good old-fashioned irony.

I push the PLAY button on my MP3 player that hangs from the windshield frame. Two speakers, strung up by 550 cord, start blasting Tool into our cramped Humvee.

"Is it hard for you to concentrate with that music playing?" asks the scared-shitless kid.

"Do you play music in your car back home?"

"Yeah."

"Trust me, man," I say. "There's a lot more to pay attention to while driving back home than there is here."

"Really?"

"Hell yeah," says Zerega from the roof. "Back home you have to watch out for other cars and stupid drivers. Here, a stupid driver is a dead driver."

He laughs that maniacal laugh of his.

"Dude, we own the road here," I tell the kid in the backseat. "Civilians have to get out of our way—"

"Or it's roast Haji for dinner!" Zerega cries. Then he rolls his tongue to make a machine gun noise.

Gasparotto and I laugh. We're used to Zerega's antics. Plus, we know he's only upping the ante today to get a rise out of this kid. Truth is nine out of ten convoys are routine and uneventful. It's not unreasonable that he's trying to invent some entertainment.

"All you have to do on a convoy is stay on the road," I tell the kid. "Especially being the last vehicle. We don't even have to know where we're going."

"Ninety-nine Hajis alive on the road! Ninety-nine Hajis alive! You shoot one dead, run over his head! Ninety-eight Hajis alive on the road!" Zerega sings.

"Don't mind him," Gasparotto tells the kid in the backseat. "He's crazy."

"Oh," says the kid.

"Trust me," I say. "You guys will be fine. And music doesn't distract you from anything. Plus, if we're going to go out, we might as well do it with a little style, right?"

The kid nods his head. I put on my aviator sunglasses and turn up the speakers.

The handheld radio crackles. It's LT.

"All Hunter elements, this is two-six. We're rollin'."

The brake lights on the vehicle ahead of me go dim, and I put the Humvee in drive. We roll out of the gate. Outside the wire.

Zerega loads his SAW once we're out. That familiar *click-clack*. Those familiar wind chimes of the devil.

"Let's kick some ass!" he yells from the roof. The way his voice echoes, the way it overcomes the steady roar of the diesel engine, it's like God talking.

Zerega is, for all intents and purposes, crazy. Out of all of us, he's developed his sick sense of humor the most. But developing humor, it's the reason we've survived. Not literally, of course. Laughing at a bomb doesn't make it any less lethal. But mentally it's the humor that keeps us going. It's how we stay strong.

See, Zerega makes some fun out of this kid's first convoy, out of this kid's fear. But it's also Zerega's fear. His fear is why he sings "Ninety-nine Hajis." Our fear is why Gasparotto and I laugh with him instead of telling him to shut up. It's why I throw on my aviators and crank the music. Going insane is how we keep our sanity.

And out of all the convoys this is the scariest. The convoy up here was pretty scary, but at that time home was a long way off, anyway. This is our last convoy, and home is just around the corner.

I drive down the road, thinking of a soldier I met while waiting at the PAX terminal to go on my two-week leave. He told me about a guy in his company who went on leave in February. While waiting at the PAX terminal, the guy got one of many Estimated Times of Departure. They had a few hours, so he decided to take a trip to the PX. He didn't really have a reason to go other than boredom, but he figured he could pick up a pack of gum or something. On his way he was hit by a mortar and killed.

Driving down the endless dirt road for what will be the last time, this is the kind of story that runs through your head. The image of a soldier whistling and skipping down a concrete sidewalk runs through my mind over and over again. All he's thinking about is how hard he'll hold his parents or kids or wife or girlfriend when he finally sees them again. Home is just around the corner for him. Just a few short traveling days and his war was over. And then, out of the sky, there's the *whoosh* of displaced air and then the *boom* of an explosion. And then there's the shrapnel slicing through his body.

Irony is a literary device that's supposed to happen in novels. It's supposed to keep the reader interested and entertained. But living in a war zone, you realize that irony is real life. To deal with it we develop a sick sense of humor.

Living in a war zone, you realize that God is the one with a sick sense of humor. So I guess that makes us Godlike.

I drive down the empty road trying to empty my mind of ironic images. There's a herd of cows off to the left edge of the road. One cow in particular seems to be the leader of the pack. She's standing at the very edge of the road waiting to cross. She's fearless, or perhaps just stupid.

The tenth vehicle in the convoy, the one right in front of me, zooms past the skinny brown cow. Somehow I know that this stupid, fearless cow won't be patient enough to allow me, the last vehicle, to pass before crossing. Irony is what I expect out of this convoy, and irony is what I get.

Like the rabbit in *Alice in Wonderland*, the cow heads into traffic. But unlike the rabbit who's "late for a very important date," the dumb cow plods along without a care in the world.

You couldn't have waited for one more damn Humvee? I think.

There is no way in hell I am going to halt an entire convoy to watch one starving Iraqi cow cross the road. Not to mention the herd behind her that now seems to admire her plodding along. They're sure to follow shortly.

I slam the gas pedal to the floor, and it becomes a race. The diesel engine roars, and the needle on the speedometer is buried. I time the cow's slow trot with my own increasing speed. Luckily, after a year of dodging every possible

IED at every possible speed, the situation is almost second nature. But, hey, you never know.

I can't see them, but I know the two replacement soldiers are jockeying for position, trying to catch a glimpse out of the windshield. It's our last convoy, and I expect to see God's sick sense of humor awaiting me with the swipe of fate's sickle. Instead, I am playing chicken with a cow. I don't know what kind of irony you'd call that, but it's something.

"Smithson!" Gasparotto yells over the deafening roar of the engine. Just like Woodlief going into the dust devil, Gasparotto grabs the "oh shit" handle in front of him.

"Can't stop now!" I yell, smiling.

Bring it on, Fate!

The cow steps across the road. Her front foot crosses the middle of the road and her head sticks out into the right lane. Since we're the last Humvee and his weapon needs to face six o'clock, Zerega is watching the road behind us. He has no idea we're about to collide with a suicidal cow.

"Hold on, Z!" I yell.

I barely hear him say "What?" as we approach the stupid cow.

I jerk the wheel to the right at the last possible second. No one in the Humvee is breathing. And the passenger side tires jump off the edge of the road. They stir the hot sand, and I wrestle with the wheel to keep the Humvee from jumping off completely.

The side mirrors on an armored Humvee stick out more than a foot, so the driver can see out of his small armored window. As we pass her, I look the cow directly in her dumb black eyes. I wait for her blood to splatter out of her nose and across my thick windshield. I wait to smack into her and feel the Humvee fly out of control. She's still plodding along, well into the right lane, and I watch the tip of her nose miss my side mirror by inches.

Zerega howls in laughter. The sudden hop off the road probably threw his heart into his throat. His laughter, I think, is of relief.

"You should've told me," Zerega yells through the hole in the roof. "I would've wasted her!"

I look in my rearview, and the cow is slowly turning around to walk back toward the herd.

You spend a whole year avoiding man-made bombs. You spend an entire year thinking that humanity's evil is going to widow your wife. The whole year, your brain is consumed with thoughts of being murdered. Then the thing that almost takes you out is some stupid, impatient cow.

Above the diesel engine I can hear God laughing at me. That maniacal laugh of his.

There's no such thing as an atheist in a foxhole.

////////////////////// **THE END** //////////////////////

"Hey, Smithson," says LT.

"Yes, sir?"

"What's the best part about being in Iraq?"

"One way or another, sir, you know you're going to leave."

"That's right," he says, smiling.

This is the last thing we say while our feet stand on Iraqi ground. As the plane lifts off of Anaconda's runway, the whole plane erupts in applause and cheering.

When we land in Kuwait, again the crowd cheers and we unload the plane. We're led to a tent where we'll be spending a few hours before our next plane takes off. Here's that familiar, windy place we remember from twelve months ago.

This camp has soldiers coming and going at all hours of the night. But no midnight chow. So, as the rest of the company stays back at the tent, EQ platoon sets off to find some food. We've been eating MREs for the last year. We would rather not eat them while we wait for the plane to take us home.

After fifteen minutes of walking we find the chow hall. It's closed, but there's a back door open. So we help ourselves. Etiquette goes out the window when you're hungry. And when you've just survived a year in Iraq.

The door leads to the kitchen. It looks recently tidied up and cleaned. So there's not much food lying around, but there is a large basket of fruit and another basket full of chips.

"Take what you can," says LT.

We're all grinning at the absurdity of stealing fruit and chips from a chow hall, but we're doing it anyway. I look at LT, and he shrugs.

"Shouldn't have left the door open," he says.

A guy comes out from the front of the chow hall. He looks like a cook. He's not military, so we pretty much ignore him.

"You guys can't be in here," he says. The look on his face is priceless. Imagine the look on a homeless man's face when you start reading the newspaper he's using for a blanket. There are more than twenty of us, and he knows he can't stop us. So we grab what we can and walk out the door.

"Thanks," Scott Moore tells him.

"This is so out of character," I say to Moore.

"Oh well."

He takes a bite out of an apple.

"Did I tell you about the last time I was in Kuwait, going home on leave?"

"I don't think so," he says.

"You told me," says Roman. "In the shower trailer?"

"Yeah," I say. Then to Moore: "You know at Camp Doha, they have those, like dozen, shower trailers lined up at the end of the tents?"

"Yeah," he says.

"The place was real busy. Tons of people going on leave . . ."

> On my way to the showers I pass a guy walking to the tents.
>
> "Go to the one all the way down at the end," he says. "There's almost no one there."
>
> "Okay, thanks," I say.
>
> And I start walking down the long length of trailers. As I pass each one, there are less and less soldiers going in and out of them. When I get to the last one, I walk up the stairs to the trailer's door.

Opening the door, I see that the whole trailer is empty. There are four or five shower stalls and four or five toilet stalls.

"All right," I say. "I got the place to myself."

I have to take a quick whiz, and I notice there are no urinals. Kind of weird, but you never know how equipped the facilities in the army are going to be. Not thinking much of it, I use one of the stalls. Then I take my time and get undressed. I start one of the showers and smile to myself in the mirror. Just a few short hours and I'll be heading home.

After a long hot shower I get out and wrap a towel around myself. I lather up and start shaving in one of the five sinks.

The door opens, and I look over to see who ruined my privacy.

It's a female.

She doesn't look in my direction, just turns and walks to one of the bathroom stalls.

I wonder if she knows she's in the wrong trailer, I think.

I look at the stalls again. There are no urinals. And then things start to click.

I'm the one in the wrong trailer. There's always a female shower trailer among the male trailers. And it's usually the one on the end. The soldier who gave

*me the advice wasn't trying to trick me. When he
said the trailer "all the way at the end," he assumed
I would go to the last male trailer.*

*I rush to put my shirt and shorts on, and I realize
my face is still half full of shaving cream. I look at
the stall to which the female went. Then I look back
in the mirror. Back and forth until I decide I might
have enough time. I don't want only half my face
shaved.*

*I run the razor over my chin and neck so fast I cut
myself twice. I throw on my shirt, stuff my toiletries
back in my little bag, and rush out the door. On my
way back to the tent I start laughing hysterically.*

"And no one ever knew the wiser," I say.

"I can't believe you did that," says Josh Roman.

"I can," says Scott Moore.

Back at the tent EQ enjoys its pirated food. Some of the
company tries to nap for the few hours we have, but we
mainly stay up. We may talk briefly about going home but
mostly we talk about the past year.

It's funny. When you're at war, all you talk about is
going home. Now that we're going home, all we talk about
is being at war.

"Man, our first time in Kuwait seems like forever ago,"

says Seabass. He's sitting on the floor across from me eating barbeque potato chips.

"I know," I say.

"All I can remember about Camp Virginia is the smell of it," says LT. "That fried, sandy smell of chow in the desert."

"The diesel fuel and grease," I say.

"How many times did we PMCS those friggin' dozers?" asks Koprowski.

"Too many," says Josh Roman.

"Hey, Smithson," says Neil Munoz from a little ways down the line of cots. "How about the smell of my shit?"

I laugh.

"I forgot about that," I say.

"Dude," says LT. "You wiping your boots off with a rock. That was one of the funniest things I've ever seen."

"What is this?" asks Zerega.

"You never heard this story?" says LT. "Oh, Smithson, you have to tell him."

"All right," I say. "Remember when Roman, LT, Munoz, and I got called for that range watching detail?"

"Yeah," says Zerega. "While we were armoring the twenty-tons."

"Yeah," I say. "Well, LT and Roman were in one Humvee and Munoz and I were in another. . . ."

Kuwait, besides for acclimatization and ship unloading, is for training. One of the training ranges is where this story takes place. We've already been to this range for unit training. And now we are back to act as security guards.

The range is a fake town. A mock convoy full of apprehensive soldiers drives through every thirty or so minutes and fires at pop-up targets. Some of the targets are angry-looking people wearing masks and holding weapons. Others are of smiling families.

The mock convoys drive through the mock town, firing at mock targets, avoiding firing at mock families, and weaving from mock IEDs. Then they park in a box formation and hold an AAR. Each convoy comes through three times. Think crawl, walk, run. The first time, crawl phase, that's a dry run. No rounds are used. The second time, walking, that's half speed, blank rounds. The third time is full speed, running with live rounds.

And then there's the range watch. On this half of the range the range watch is Munoz and I. We sit three hundred meters away from the fake town in our Humvee watching the desert be flat. Really we're watching for safety reasons. And by safety reasons, I mean camels. Plus, sure, if someone gets shot, we have a handheld radio to contact range control.

But mostly we're here for camel watching.

LT and Roman are off toward the beginning of the range. Two whole days. Guess how many camels. You got it. Not a one. So we take turns between dozing off and watching the route.

There's nothing around for miles but the range and a six-foot sign that says RANGE 2. We're parked right next to the latter. It's December, and it's pretty cold out. During the day it's about fifty degrees, and during the night, it gets down around thirty. And that damn wind, it never stops. Though, because we sit in a Humvee all day, the elements are tolerable.

"Oh, man," says Munoz. "I gotta shit."

He shifts around in his seat trying to hold it in. For some reason no one has thought to place a port-a-john at the range watching point. That's the army for you. Eleven hours of sitting in a Humvee, munching MREs, and no toilet.

"Better hold it," I say.

I put my nose back into a book. And he does hold it, but there are six more hours out here. So he gives up. A convoy just drove through the mock village and sits three hundred meters to our left holding their AAR. I am the driver, and we face the desert so that the passenger side of the Humvee can't be seen by the parked convoy.

"All right, I'm going for it," announces Munoz.

"Have a good one," I say.

You always keep toilet paper in a Humvee. Golden rule. So Munoz grabs the roll and glances out my window to make sure the convoy is still parked. He opens his door and squats on the passenger side. He holds the edge of his door and uses it to brace himself so he can sit like in a chair. All I can see is his head out of the backseat passenger's window. So I think his boom-boom will end up somewhere next to that door.

He finishes up and pulls himself back into his seat.

"I can't believe you just did that, Sergeant," I say.

"Gotta do what you gotta do," he says. "Just watch out on this side. I pushed some dirt over it, so don't step on the mound."

After a few more boring hours of reading, napping, and getting to know Munoz, I have to pee. The wind blows from the left, where another convoy has rolled through, camel free, and is parked in a box formation at the end of the mock town. So I stand at the rear of the Humvee with my back to the wind so as to avoid spray-back. Peeing into the wind is a mistake you make only once.

Munoz leans his head out of his window.

"Watch out for my shit," he says.

"All right," I say, looking down at the small mound of dirt on the ground outside the back passenger seat.

I laugh and continue my stream. When I'm done, I shake off and button my pants. I look out over the flat, brown desert. Seeing the curve of the earth makes me laugh and shake my head. I decide I want a cigarette. Now, I don't really smoke, but this is a stupidly dull detail. Smoking is something to do besides read and nap.

People wonder why soldiers smoke. This is why: because two days of range watching is enough boredom for your whole life.

I pull the lighter from my pocket and try to burn the cigarette hanging from my mouth. The wind blows hard, and the lighter's flame won't stay up. I turn my back to the wind and try some more. This still doesn't work.

The Humvee is built like a sort of pickup truck. The wind rushes right over the back half. So with my back to the wind I move to the left, finding cover behind the taller, rear passenger seat.

With the cigarette lit I stand up and gaze at the curve of the brown earth. I inhale a few times.

Iraq can't be this boring, *I think.*

I fuss around like people do when they're bored, when they're smoking. I shift weight from one foot to the other and twist my feet in the dirt.

Uh-oh, *I think.* Please tell me it's farther left.

I slowly lower my stare to my feet. There between them is light, desert brown sand swirled like ice cream with dark, Munoz brown shit. I lift my feet and look at the bottoms. The treads are packed with sticky, recycled army chow.

I look around for a place to wipe it off. The only thing around besides the Humvee is the Range 2 sign. It stands off to my right like a pillar. It's a pretty large sign supported by four by four posts. On one of these posts is where I rub my shit-covered soles.

Munoz sees me and pokes his head out of his window. Then he looks back at the trampled mound he made. His laugh is hearty, from the belly, just like his crap.

"You stupid ass," he says.

I wipe my boots off the best I can on the Range 2 signpost.

When we get back to the range control station, where we sleep in the Humvees, we meet up with LT and Roman. Of course Munoz is eager to tell

the story as I pour water on my boot and scrape the
treads with a pointy rock I found.

"So LT's about to fall over laughing—"

"And then"—LT takes over the storytelling—"Smithson says, 'You eat corn yesterday, Sergeant Munoz?' I don't think I've ever laughed so hard in my life!"

LT wipes the tears out of his eyes.

Soon the company is led outside to another runway. This time, we board a commercial plane, like the one on which we came over. Instead of Germany, this time we refuel in Ireland. Then we board the plane that will take us to Fort Bragg.

The moon shines out the window. The waves in the Atlantic break up the moonlight, making it dance around thirty thousand feet below us. There are a few overhead lights on in the plane, the ones you use to read, that give some of the cabin an orange glow. Most of the plane is sleeping, dreaming of home. A bunch of us from EQ platoon, we stay up.

We reminisce about the year we wished away, the year that would never end, the year that's over now.

"LT," says Marc Zerega, "you want to talk about falling over hilarious. What about the time on the Samarra mission?"

"With Smithson?" asks LT.

Zerega nods.

"Oh my God. I haven't thought about that in months."

"What happened on the Samarra mission?" asks Jesse Smith.

"That's right, he wasn't here yet," says Zerega.

Smith and a few other guys joined our unit about half-way through the tour. So they weren't there for the Samarra mission.

"Why don't you tell this one, sir?" I say to LT.

"So this was the mission when you guys got ambushed?" asks Smith.

"Actually I think it was the same night we got ambushed," says Zerega.

"Yeah," says LT. "In the tent at FOB Summerall. I walk in and a bunch of guys are in the back by Zerega's cot. . . ."

It's after dinner. No one can sleep, so we're up telling riddles. LT comes in the tent, bags under his eyes, and joins our group.

I stand up to meet LT and say, "Sir, a farmer has twenty sick sheep. One dies. How many does he have left?"

When you ask someone this riddle, they'll say twenty-five sheep until they're blue in the face. Because out loud, when you say "twenty sick sheep," it sounds like "twenty-six sheep."

LT doesn't know the answer, so he just keeps walking. Now, he's 6'2" and I'm 5'6". So as he walks, he has to look down. And since you don't stand toe-to-toe with an officer, I have to back up. He gets police-interrogation close and stares me down, grinning the whole time.

"Sir, I'm going to need an answer," I tell him.

He keeps walking.

"I'm warning you, LT," I say.

When we're ten feet away from the original group, I feel something brewing down below. It's just unnecessary for LT to still be towering over me with this shit-eating grin he's wearing, so I do something about it.

I turn quickly so my butt is facing him. Then I let out a little fart, a tiny squeaker. Think of a rabbit burping.

When I turn back to face him, LT has stopped dead in his tracks. The group explodes in laughter.

"Push" is all LT says.

I get down in the front leaning rest and start knocking them out. From the group Zerega says, "You don't fart on a commissioned officer in the U.S. army!"

LT says he needs a spot to sit and contemplate the

answer to my riddle. That's when I get flattened on the wooden floor.

"I didn't say stop," he says. I make a feeble attempt to push with him sitting on my back.

"Recover, Smithson," he says when he gets off me. "You know, they put you through a lot of training classes when you become an officer. What to do when one of your soldiers farts on you? Not one of them."

"That's because the army never saw me coming, sir."

"I can't even be mad at you, Smithson," he says. "You were desperate. And that, my friend, was a brilliant solution. You looked like a squid shooting your ink."

"You called me Squidy for two weeks," I say.

"I wouldn't expect anything less from you, Smithson," says Jesse Smith.

"Hey," says Todd Wegner, who joined our little EQ huddle when he heard the farting-on-LT story. "Remember when the commander came out on that mission?"

"Yeah," I say, laughing quietly so I don't wake up the rest of the people on the plane, who all seem to be sleeping.

"And he set his cot up on the edge of the tent?" says LT. He covers his mouth with one hand, and all I can see are his eyes. On top of the dark bags his eyes laugh with all the force his mouth can't right now.

"I gotta hear this one," says Jesse Smith.

"All right," I say. "Well, in the wintertime, all it does in Iraq is rain. . . ."

The tent at FOB Summerall has plywood floors. This is so the puddles of rain and mud that collect outside the tent don't come inside the tent. But apparently these tents were set up during the dry season because there's slack in the tent's roof. So every night when it rains, the edges pool with water until they leak. Obviously, after only one night of sleeping here, we figure out to place our cots in the center of the tent and leave the edges clear.

During the second week of the Samarra mission the commander comes out to the field with us. He walks in the tent, and you can almost hear the sigh let loose from everyone's mouth. The commander is wearing his tan army-issue gloves. Outside of his office he always wears gloves. His uniform is pressed and sparkling clean. And his body armor and field gear look like they were just pulled from their plastic packaging.

It hasn't started raining yet, and the commander begins setting up a cot. Instead of taking a hint or—here's a thought—asking someone, he sets his cot up on the outskirts of the thirty others pushed toward the tent's center. He must assume we all pushed our cots together because we enjoy the smell of one another's feet and morning breath. Though I'm sure he thinks we pushed our cots to the center to give him more living space. While he wrestles with the cumbersome army cot, no one offers him a hand or bothers to tell him that the edges of the tent drip rainwater all night.

The commander is the first one asleep, and it doesn't start raining until one in the morning. We're woken up by his lone, key chain flashlight as it dances blue light across the tent.

Sticking my head out of my sleeping bag, I see him trying to keep the little LED's button pushed down with one hand and move his stuff with the other. I turn back over to go to sleep.

Quietly, head in my sleeping bag, I laugh because it's the middle of the night in a combat zone. . . .

"And the commander took the time to put on his gloves," I finish.

When we land in Fort Bragg, the applause is deafening. EQ platoon sits in the back of the plane laughing and cheering. We pat each other on the back and shake each other's hands. And the whole time, in all of our eyes, that look of regret. The same one I gave Heather. There's that shameful feeling of abandonment.

This time I'm not leaving the love of my life for a year. I'm leaving my only brothers and one sister forever. Even if the unit gets deployed again, the half of the platoon that was cross-leveled won't be cross-leveled back. The army just doesn't work like that.

Back in Old Division Area, we settle down into the barracks the same way we did while we were going through mobilization training.

The first night the whole platoon is taking turns in and out of the bath and shower room. I stand next to Justin Greene and Austin Rhodes at the sink, brushing my teeth. I look in the mirror, and my eyes are desperate.

When I was here the first time, I was desperate because I wanted to be brave. Now "brave" means nothing. All I want to do is hold on to that year. I don't necessarily want to return to Iraq. And I sure as hell want to go home and see my family, but in the last few days of something you know will never come back, your mind has a desperate way of holding on to it.

"Remember when you got your wisdom teeth pulled?" Greene asks Rhodes through the minty suds in his mouth.

"Yeah, all four of them," says Rhodes, spitting into his sink.

"I remember that," says Jesse Lee, standing a few sinks

down. "And Smithson had to watch him."

"Had to?" I say. "I volunteered for that. It was hilarious. . . ."

"Somebody has to stay back with him," says Munoz.

"I'll stay back," I offer immediately. How can I turn this down?

"All right, we'll bring you guys a plate," says Jesse Lee.

Normally dentists won't pull all four wisdom teeth in one shot, but this is the army and we are in a combat zone. There's no time for mercy.

However Rhodes doesn't feel the slightest ounce of pain. He's still drugged from whatever they gave him at the dentist. Though "drugged" may not be the right adjective. Downright royally stoned seems more appropriate.

Rhodes sits in a chair in our common room, the one with the shelf full of candy, in a drunken slumped position. His head is back, jaw open, and the clump of gauze in the back of his mouth makes it difficult for him to talk.

"No tea-bagging Rhodesh," he says.

The whole group of us is laughing when LT walks by. He looks down at Rhodes slumped there in his inebriated state and smiles.

"You feelin' okay, buddy?" asks LT.

"You arn gonna tea-bag me are you, shir?"

LT laughs and assures Rhodes that no tea-bagging of any sort will occur. Then the group heads off to chow.

Minus two, that is. Rhodes and I sit in the common room, next to the fridge, and he tells me all about how he'd fought to stay awake while the dentist intravenously knocked him out.

"I don think itsch werrkin'," he had told the dentist. The dentist prepped another needle and gave him a second dose. "Then my head juss fell back and I passhed owt." Rhodes fakes his head falling back and almost falls out of the chair. This is why he needs a guardian while the rest go to lunch.

I catch him and lift him back into his seat.

"Thanksch," he mutters.

He looks to the platoon's dry erase board, which sits on the wall beside him. It has all the soldiers from EQ listed by last name. There are small corresponding boxes for writing in where they are at any given time. It's for accountability.

Rhodes turns in his chair, grabs the marker, and begins scribbling things next to the names of those who had just gone to chow. Normally, we write a D for DFAC (Dining Facility) when we go to chow. Rhodes just writes "food."

"I need a shmoke," he tells me.

"I don't think you should be smoking," I say.

"Doctor shaid itsh okay ash long ash the gauze esh there," he informs me. "Maybe Fawldeh hash shome shigarettesh."

"He's at chow," I say.

Rhodes apparently doesn't believe me and stumbles out of his chair to prove me wrong.

"Be careful," I tell him.

"For wha?"

He staggers through the nearby doorway to the hallway and Folden's room. Knocking on the door, he asks for Sergeant Folden.

"He's at chow," I say again. Rhodes opens the door and enters the room.

"Surjen Fawldeh?" he asks the empty room.

This room is the size of a cubicle and to anyone except Rhodes obviously unoccupied. I stand at the doorway chuckling as Rhodes pats down Folden's bedsheets.

"He'sh not shleepin."

I try to remain polite and avoid just laughing at him, but when I see him physically pat down a bed to be sure no one is sleeping in it, I lose it.

"Yoush okay, mahn?" he asks me.

"I'm fine," I say. "Let's go to your room and sit down."

We walk back into the hallway and down to his bay.

"Wanna shee the tooths that got pulled?" he asks me.

"Sure," I say.

He pulls a small plastic jar from a nearby shelf. Inside are four bloody teeth.

"Look at thish one." He points. The tooth he refers to has a gnarly, pointed chunk sticking out of its side, not unlike the barb on the edge of a fishhook. "Thatsh gonna hurt when it comesh out."

"Yeah," I agree. He puts the teeth down and sets up to play me in Battlefield 1942 on his laptop. Sadly he kicks my ass.

After a little while Jesse Lee comes back with the crowd and gives us our to-go plates. I have a hamburger and onion rings. Rhodes gets peaches and some Jell-o. He takes the bloody gauze out of his mouth. Then, after more than a few unsuccessful tries, he pokes his fork into a peach slice.

"Ish thish my lower lip?" he asks us with his finger on his lower lip. We tell him yes, and he places the peach there. Tipping his head back, he opens and

closes his mouth. Think of a seal trying to swallow a
dead fish. I guess he's hoping gravity will help him
out and shimmy the peach into his mouth.

Lee and I stand in the doorway watching him.
Our laughs start as scratchy grunts in the back of our
throats. Again, attempting to save his dignity, we
try to keep the laughs from becoming audible.

After a couple of jaw flexes the peach falls right into
Rhodes's lap. And his dignity falls with it, because as
it sits on his pants, Rhodes keeps opening and closing
his mouth, attempting to eat the slippery thing.

Lee and I roar with laughter. Rhodes looks at us
like a lost puppy. Then down at the peach slice in his
lap. Then, as he tries to poke it with the fork, I say,
"Sorry, man."

Although I'm still laughing. So I have to say it a
few more times before he actually believes me.

"Rhodes ate the rest of his meal in front of a mirror,"
I say.

After a week of out-processing we are all flying out from
the airport in Raleigh, North Carolina. Before we head
to the holding area (also in Old Division Area) where the
buses come to take us to the airport, the commander lines
us up in formation.

In Iraq, because of the danger of mortars, we couldn't hold formations. With the whole company lined up one well-placed mortar could wipe out a whole platoon. So being in formation at Fort Bragg, although we're in the army, is a pretty foreign thing.

However, we don't forget our little twist on the commander's attempt at motivation and morale. Every time he calls us to attention, we're supposed to yell, "Adapt and overcome."

We're all lined up, standing at ease. The commander comes to the front with his head high.

"Company!" he yells.

"Platoon!" yells Munoz.

Then the commander: "Attention."

The whole company says his quirky little line. EQ platoon cries out what we always say: "Inept and overdone."

We all grin as we stand at attention. This is our last little attempt of holding on to the year, the last time we get to do something as a platoon, the last time we get to use our sense of humor, the biting sarcasm that got us through our year in Iraq.

All of our planes take off at different times, so every couple of hours the buses come and load a bunch of us at a time. We're all trying so hard not to cry. No one offers to shake a hand, because you're supposed to hug your brothers and sisters.

// SILENCE AND SILHOUETTES //

When you come home from a combat tour, the veteran's association lets you collect unemployment benefits for a few months. It's so you can have time to readjust, to get back on your feet.

Sitting on my own couch again while Heather is at work, I watch daytime TV. I'm not really watching, though. Daytime TV sucks. And my mind has never been further from home.

Seeing Heather at the airport was magical. Seeing my parents again, indescribable. Their tears, their hugs of joy. Their fears are finally over. They hold me like they're never going to let me go.

And my life can finally begin moving again. For a whole

year plans stood still. No college. No career. All the people with whom I graduated high school are finishing up their two-year degrees. I'm just starting my first semester in January. With my return home from Iraq I can finally start playing catch-up. Heather and I can start saving for a house. We can start talking about having kids, of being able to settle down.

But my mind is far away.

I think of the war. I think of all the kids still over there, still living in the middle of all the violence. I think of all the soldiers fighting that same, tired battle. But mostly I think of EQ platoon. And I know they're thinking of me. After all, they're the only ones who can understand our little slice of military history. They're the only ones who can understand the feeling of your life being on hold, like a school-yard bully is dangling it just out of your reach. And they're the only ones who can understand how selfish we were for wishing it all away.

I know now that Andy Zeltwanger was wrong. The best part about being in Iraq is not that, one way or another, you'll be leaving. The best part about being in Iraq is the platoon who's there with you.

I think of one particular memory, a peaceful memory. I'm sitting in the motor pool with Seabass. Just sitting there outside the barracks. It's late dusk. The very end of a day. The very beginning of a night.

The desert is so calm at night. Calmer than anything I can remember. It's not hot anymore. The temperature has dropped, and it actually feels cool. A dry, comfortable coolness, like nighttime in late August at home.

Even on camp, there's no noise, just the sound of our breathing. We don't talk. Sebastian and I sit together in silence, like you'd do with a friend you've known your whole life. We'd been talking, I'm sure, about something. Probably something funny. We were probably joking about the commander, or one of the squad leaders, or one of life's little ironic lessons. But now things are silent.

We light cigarettes and look out over the motor pool. The only light comes from a single "porch" light outside the company's CQ. The sky as usual shines a curious gray-orange. Sand in the air. Always sand in the air. No moon is out, just dust. This country is beautiful.

The shadows of the dozens of pieces of equipment in our motor pool pierce the orange glow. Tall outlines of dump trucks, of hydraulic excavators with their long gangly arms, of scrapers and dozers and a fuel truck and those unforgettable M916 tractor trailers. Their silhouettes slice open the gray-orange. They remind me of headstones in a cemetery. Dark and silent and eerie. A filthy, taunting bit of foreshadowing . . . or just coincidence.

We inhale smoke into our lungs and breathe it out. We're thankful to breathe, thankful to have the choice to breathe smoke. We say nothing, not about the captain or the army, not about the mission coming up or our families.

We just sit, appreciating this moment of peace, appreciating each other.

And I realize I love Sebastian Koprowski. I realize I love every member of EQ platoon. It's a weird sort of love. Certainly not like lovers. And not like good friends. Not even like brothers, though that is how we refer to one another. I love Seabass like a buddy, an army buddy. It's a love that can't be explained. It's a fragile sort of love that loses meaning the more I complicate it with words.

Next to us is a pile of new tires. We could sit inside the barracks or out on the deck where our platoon meetings are held, called the BOHICA (Bend Over, Here It Comes Again). We could hang out with the rest of the guys. But we don't. Instead we sit here next to tires, watching the calm, cool desert. We appreciate the night, the life, the love. We appreciate the silence and silhouettes.

There's an explosion. Not anywhere near. Somewhere in the distance. Miles across the huge camp. We don't look at each other, and we don't break stride in inhaling the smoke.

Another explosion. Surely they are mortars; we've heard them hundreds of times before. But we don't care anymore. We enjoy the silence in between.

"I wonder how long it'll be until they sound the alarm," I say.

My brother smirks. The statement is tired and overused. We all understand how much of a joke the mortar alarms are.

Another explosion. Another inhale.

The explosions are far away. Think of the fading echo of fireworks. They're silent like death is silent.

"Imagine if the five-ton got hit," he says.

We often fantasize about losing parked equipment to mortar damage. We are hopeful, but it probably won't happen. We're not that lucky.

After another explosion there is a long pause before the alarm sounds. It's a good five minutes after the first explosion. What the hell's the use? That goddamn alarm, always disrupting a good time.

After a final inhale Seabass turns and says, "Wanna head in?"

"Yeah, let Renninger know we're not dead."

Sitting here on my couch, I can hear him laugh through his nose.

I think of hugging him when we left Fort Bragg. I think of leaving EQ platoon. I think of abandoning them.

I am glad to be home, for sure, but, really, the hardest part of going to war is you have to go back home. Culture shock doesn't begin to describe a trip home from the Middle East, that other planet.

I spend a year there. I am just a kid, a Joe Schmo of the

masses, and I've seen things some people will never see. My memories of the war, of EQ platoon, they'll save me. But my memories will also haunt me.

Psychologists call it post-traumatic stress disorder.

The acronym, PTSD, won't get out of my head. I sit on the couch, not watching daytime TV, and I remember being at Fort Bragg. I remember the sergeant telling us all what to expect when we get home. Readjustment, that's what he calls it. PTSD, that's a diagnosis, he tells us. The way he says diagnosis, it makes PTSD sound like a disease. PTSD *is* a disease, he says.

Ever wonder if there's a little cancer cell living inside you? Ever wonder if there's nothing you can do about it?

That's like sitting on this couch.

I think of that stupid PTSD briefing, that stupid readjustment speech. I think of that active duty soldier asking us how we'll deal with facing our family again. EQ platoon just gives him blank stares. We don't know. I remember the dumb, dark eyes of a cow crossing traffic.

This is a room full of soldiers I just spent a year with in a combat zone. Every day our lives were in danger. Now, in a matter of days, we're going to be ripped apart and sent home to families who can't possibly understand.

"What will you say to your mother, your child, your wife when they say, 'You know, I'm really upset that you're still in the military'?" asks the readjustment expert.

"So am I," I say.

My response breaks the blank stares, and the room erupts in laughter. Then, pretending to be my family again, he asks me, "'Well, then, honey, why are you still in?'"

"Because it's our duty," someone says.

And that's it.

We are on American soil again, for God's sake. The last things we care about are flashbacks and nightmares. We've been through a certain degree of hell, and we can tough out some petty psychological trauma.

Ever wonder if that little cancer cell will decide to multiply? Ever wonder how all those cancer cells will finally show themselves?

That's what waking up in the middle of the night is like.

My eyes pop open. I don't move a muscle. I was not having a nightmare, but my breath is way too labored for the middle of the night. My heart is ready to explode. My face is coated in sweat. I am absolutely terrified, and I have no idea why.

We live in the country, and the night is still and quiet. It's quiet like death. Think of a cemetery. Think of cancer cells multiplying.

There's a red laser light shining on the ceiling. It's from the alarm clock that sits on my nightstand. It says 2:25 A.M. The bedroom door is cracked, and yellow light from a night-light in the hallway slips through. The way I'm breathing, the way my heart feels the size of a watermelon, it's what dying must feel like.

I am petrified, and what's scarier is I don't know why. I've never woken up in the middle of the night for no reason. In Iraq fear was commonplace, sure, but never while you were sleeping. Never for no reason. We got used to being afraid. We got so used to it that it wasn't even fear we were dealing with. It was just humor.

Now lying in my bed, nothing has ever seemed less humorous. I'm on American soil, no reason to fear anything, and my heart pounds like a bass drum. I wipe the sweat off my forehead and turn over to find a more comfortable position. Turning over puts my back to the door.

I need to watch that door, I think. *Someone is coming to kill me.*

I turn back over and close my eyes, trying to stop the pounding in my chest, the labored breaths.

I need to watch that door.

And my eyes pop open.

You're acting crazy, I tell myself as I watch the door. *You're in West Sand Lake, New York. People don't go around just killing each other. Some people don't even lock their doors.*

That reminds me, *I should check the front door.*

I get out of bed. Heather is sound asleep. I need to protect her, too. I walk to the entrance of our apartment. The doorknob is locked. The dead bolt is locked. The chain is secure. I check again, just to be sure.

Go back to bed and quit being paranoid, I whisper. *You're not in Iraq. No one's trying to kill you.*

I crawl back into bed. I toss and turn for five minutes. I'm not tired at all. My mind races. That four-letter fucking acronym. PTSD.

Ryan, you've been home for over a month. Let it go.

I lie on my back watching the dim yellow light shine through the crack in the door. I watch and wait for the door to burst open and reveal my murderer. This feeling of terror, it's so genuine, like a sixth sense, and no amount of logic can help me escape from it. I contemplate crying, but that just seems useless. What does crying ever really do for us? It doesn't solve our problems. It doesn't make us run faster or shoot better. If anything, crying just delays the solution to our problems.

Someone's coming to kill me.

What if this isn't PTSD? What if it feels like a sixth sense because it is a sixth sense? What if I'm having an authentic ESP experience, and someone really is going to break in and kill Heather and me while we sleep?

Get a weapon, I think.

We turned in our M16s at Bragg.

I get out of bed again and go to the kitchen. I pull a butcher knife from the block on the counter. I study it for a long time. It's long and shiny and lethal. It will no doubt do the job. I'll just keep it on the nightstand next to me and use it only if I need to, only if this really is an accurate premonition.

Then I remember those horror stories of men returning home from war and murdering their wives in the bed next to them.

Is this how it starts? I ask myself. *What happens when I wake up the second time?*

I put the knife down and return to bed. I need to sleep, and no one is coming to kill me. I doze off briefly before I wake up in a cold sweat. The red laser light reads 2:37 A.M.

I need to protect myself. I need to protect my wife.

Get a fucking weapon.

I rummage through the entire house. My heart is rapid, my palms are sweaty and shaking, and not a moment goes by that I'm not checking over both shoulders. There has to be something I can use that won't be lethal unless I absolutely need it to be.

In the spare bedroom there are drumsticks for the electronic drum set Heather bought me for my birthday. I pick them up and give them a test swing. They are solid and blunt and could surely do the job. I took lessons for three years in high school, and the drumsticks feel natural and controlled in my hands. Isn't that what weapons are all about: control?

They will do.

If, God forbid, I pummel Heather, hopefully I can stop before it's too late.

Is this how it starts?

It doesn't matter. This is life and death. I take them back to the bedroom, place them next to the alarm clock, and don't sleep more than a wink all night.

I look this up online the next day. It's called a night terror. And there's no way I'm talking to some shrink about it. There's no way I'm talking to anyone about it. I don't tell Heather. I don't tell my parents or my sister. I ignore it.

And it happens again the next week. And again a few days later. For a few months this is my routine: a jolting snap from regular sleep and that terrible feeling of dying.

By the last couple of occurrences I am able to retain my sanity quickly and get back to sleep. But I just want them to stop.

The last time the night terrors occur, I wake up once again in a cold, throbbing sweat. I pray for the night terrors to end and the shame that goes along with keeping it all a secret.

What happens next will baffle me for the rest of my life.

I lie on my back watching the door. I breathe deep, trying to ignore the throbbing sound of my heartbeat. The crack in the door is about a foot wide tonight. I watch it intently.

Go to sleep. Go to sleep. Go to sleep.

My eyes shut, or maybe they stay open. There's the

lighted crack in the door, but maybe I'm dreaming.

A sharp silhouette appears in the bedroom in front of the doorway. It's slender looking and appears to have long straight hair. It's undoubtedly female. She walks toward my side of the bed.

The cold sweat reappears on my forehead.

She gets closer. I can't see her face, for the light is behind her. But I can tell she's looking me directly in the eyes, or directly to my soul.

I am paralyzed. In front of me stands what must be the reason behind these awful night terrors, and she's getting closer. My heart is pounding and my whole body is numb and tingly.

She's right next to me when she bends down. She walks, or floats maybe, down to me.

My eyes open. Or maybe they were open the whole time.

And, as if by magic, my heart slows down, and my cold sweat dries. I breathe normally. I'm no longer dizzy or tingly.

Whatever or whoever the silhouette was, it changes me, it heals me. I am perfectly calm. I lie in disbelief, but I no longer fear going back to sleep.

I have not had a night terror since.

////////// WORDS ON PAPER //////////

The hardest part of a combat tour is not the combat. It's not the year or more away from home and family. It's not sleeping in Humvees or eating MREs. It's not the desert sun that makes everything too hot to touch. It's not the fear and wild atrocity you experience. You get used to all that. Bombs are just bombs. Blood is just blood.

The hardest part of a combat tour, I've discovered, is coming home.

Not in the literal sense, of course. The bounce and squeal of our airplane tires on an American runway are the sweetest sounds these ears have ever heard. That part of coming home is easy. But dealing with the many thousands of emotions that ensue after a year in Iraq is difficult.

We act tough in PTSD briefings, but we really need them. Upon returning, the way I deal with my war stories, my silhouettes, is with silence.

I don't talk to anyone about the tour. Not Mom. Not Heather. Not even my own father. He wants to know things. He wants to know how close his son was to death. Not morbidly, not with a sick fascination. He sees me as a man. He wants to talk to me like one.

He tosses me a beer, and we sit in the back room of his garage. The poker table is on our right. There's a dart board on the wall and a foosball table that sits quietly, waiting for some playtime. There are pictures of the Adirondacks and various camping and sporting equipment.

It smells like pine and musk in this place. All man, all the time. This is somewhere I should be comfortable sharing my experiences, talking like a man. We stand by the black mini fridge and crack open our beers. I am silent, far away. My dad wants to talk.

"I'm glad you're home, son," he says, trying to sound like he's not choking on tears.

"Me too, Dad," I say, taking a sip of beer. "Me too."

More silence.

"I missed you so much, Ryan."

He puts his arm around me. I put mine around him and we stand holding each other. We both want to cry, but neither of us wants to be the first to do it. Foolish pride, I guess. That's what you get with fathers and sons.

"If you ever need to talk about anything, Ryan, you know I'm always here," he says.

"Yeah, I know, Dad," I say. "Thanks."

But I don't want to talk. My father knows that. He doesn't want to pry too hard. So we take another sip and head inside.

Mom is with Heather. We all stand in the kitchen. The same kitchen where my mother made most of my childhood dinners. In high school I'd yell at her, tell her I had to cut weight for wrestling. Or I'd tell her "No thanks" and go out with my friends. She'd put my portion in the fridge for leftovers. Then she'd watch me shut the door behind myself.

"Ready for dinner, honey?" she asks me when Dad and I walk in.

"Yeah, Mom," I say. "Smells great."

And she smiles.

Mom and Dad: the only two people on the planet who have forgiven me and supported me in everything I've done. They've dealt with bad report cards and a noisy drum set in my bedroom. They've gone to every wrestling match they could. They've seen me off at hotels and airports when the army takes me away from them.

After realizing my freedom in basic training and seeing

the starving children in Iraq, I have learned to become so grateful for their influence and support in my life. It's been a long road, one full of mistakes and regret, but I am so thankful that they never gave up, that when I blew off the dinner Mom made, she'd understand, she'd still smile. She'd still say, "I love you."

"Ryan, were you ever in combat?" Mom asks me at the dinner table. This is something she's asked before, over the phone while I was still in Iraq. I give her the same answer I did then.

"Do you really want to know?" I ask.

It's my way of telling her yes. It's a way I know won't provoke any more questioning. I gave her this response when I was in Iraq because I didn't think she really needed to hear all the gory details of war, not while I was still stuck in it. She worried enough about me. She didn't need details to scare her even more. I was looking out for her, just like she'd done for me for so many years.

Now, though, I don't have that excuse, and she knows it.

"It's okay now," she says. "You're home."

"Until my next tour," I say.

This statement shoots straight up her spine and into her tear ducts. She sees that combat, though something that is currently far away, is still a close part of my reality. I'm still in the army. And she sees that I don't want to talk about it. My father already knows this. He washes down some pork with a sip of beer.

"Yeah," says Mom. "That's true."

My parents want me to open up, but being the understanding people that they are, they refuse to step any further into my minefield. I'm not sure if it's fear of what they might find, if I'll end up exploding. They look into my eyes and they see dark secrets. They know there are parts of me that may never come out.

My father remembers talking to his grandfather about World War II. Gramps rarely talked about it, but when they sat in the VFW among other vets and a few beers deep, he opened up. My father loved when Gramps talked about the war. Even though the stories were thirty years old and even though it seemed to bother him sometimes to tell them, the stories were entertaining and exciting.

My father looks at me now with that same degree of hope. The hope that I'll loosen up and share with him what I've seen and what I've learned. Not the blood and guts; he can get that on the evening news. Dad wants to know the lessons I learned from such a unique, worldly encounter. He wants to know what I was thinking about in my bunk at night. He wants to know if I remembered the first time he took me skiing.

"Is that what you thought about, Ryan?" he wants to ask.

He wants to know what it feels like to attach ammunition to my chest and roll out of a gate in a cheaply armored truck.

"Weren't you scared?" He wants to understand the life of a soldier. *"Is it the same as when Gramps was in the navy?"*

He steps through my minefield with these questions. Each a possible trigger. He doesn't want to ask pointed, direct questions. But he wants to know.

And I wish I had the strength to answer.

Little do I know, literature is what will set me free.

See, I've always seen books as an escape. I read almost every night in Iraq, because every night I tried to get away. I would lay my military flashlight across my chest. The flashlight's red glow illuminated the pages. Up and down the light went, rising and falling with my breath.

It would turn the white pages into a shade of dark pink. The letters would become golden brown shadows, and the words formed by the these letters would resemble something alive and moving.

Every book was alive as I read it, lying in my sleeping bag. I wasn't in the godforsaken Middle East fighting a war. I was in my own country: a country of the mind.

I wasn't a soldier, a GI Joe Schmo. I was the words on paper.

The smell of a book is the best part of reading, because it makes the escape tangible. Each has a different aroma, and the smell always seems to reflect the story. *20,000 Leagues Under the Sea* by Jules Verne smells like cold metal and sea salt. A faint aroma of old cigarette smoke and playing cards rises from the pages of *Hearts in Atlantis* by Stephen King. And even in the blazing hot sun, I could smell the pure white chill of the Arctic as I turned the pages of *Deception Point* by Dan Brown.

Each book provided an escape. Each in its own way reminded me that there was much more to life that I had yet to experience. Each gave me hope and faith that I would experience more in my life.

High school defines literature with terminology: metaphors, similes, imagery.

But experience defines literature as more than words on paper. Not just escape, but more important, words that have the power to heal.

I am in my second semester of college before I even think about writing down my experiences. For a whole year I've avoided talking about the year I spent at war. And this means I've hidden from writing about it.

In English Composition II my professor gives us an essay assignment. It's a creative writing piece in which we have to describe a time when we saw something destroyed. I sit in my seat looking over the handout she gave us. It's printed on yellow paper.

"Minimum three pages," it says. "Double spaced, Times New Roman, 12-pt. font."

I read and reread the last line.

". . . saw something destroyed."

The phrase sticks out at me like a knife. Like the barrel of a hand-me-down Kalashnikov from the Cold War. Like Haji trying to kill me with it.

Something destroyed. That's exactly what happened in Iraq. The bombs and blood and guts, sure. But more than that. It was *my* destruction.

So I sit down to write a three-page paper about one of my missions in Iraq. My fingers move across the keyboard in the community college library faster than I've ever seen them do before. The story just pours out of me. No effort at all, like the story was just waiting to be told.

Pausing for a breath, I scroll back through what I just wrote. It's over twelve pages long. And I feel like I could write two hundred more.

Over the next week or so I edit and re-edit the essay. Leaving just the meat of the story, I finally cut it down to eight pages. But still, something's not quite right. I read it over again, trying to find what's missing.

Then it hits me. I need a theme. I need to show what was really destroyed. Not just the bombs. Not just the death. I need to show what was destroyed within me.

I realize that it's the innocence of my childhood that was really lost over there in the vile, churning stomach of Iraq. And it's the soldiers with whom I lost it who really understand.

So I weave a nursery rhyme into the essay. I modify the nursery rhyme so it fits with the theme of war, the theme of Iraq. And I call the piece "The Town That Achmed Built."

My professor reads our first drafts and makes comments.

"Ryan," she says to the class typing away in the computer lab. "Your turn."

I get up from my computer and go to her desk.

"Is eight pages too long?" I ask.

"No, it's fine," she says, taking the essay. "Have a seat."

She begins reading the piece. I see her back straighten when she reads the phrase, "dismembered people."

When she's done reading, she places the paper on her desk and says, "Ryan, this is amazing."

"Thank you," I say. She doesn't even know it, but she's the first person to read it.

"If you don't mind my asking," she says, "are you seeking any sort of therapy?"

I shake my head. Then I point to the essay.

"That's my therapy," I say.

She smiles.

"At the end of the semester I have the students take turns reading one of their essays," she says. "Would you mind reading this?"

"I don't know," I say, butterflies suddenly flying around inside my stomach.

"Think about it," she says.

That night I give the essay to Heather. She reads it, tears up, and says thank you.

"It means a lot to me, Ryan," she says. "That you shared that with me."

I nod, and she hugs me.

"Well," I say. "Sharing stories is the point of having them."

At the end of the semester, when my turn comes around, I read "The Town That Achmed Built" to a class full of college kids. Before the first paragraph is over I'm sniffling and talking through tears.

I take a deep breath and look to my professor. She nods her head, urging me to continue.

While I read, I can't look up from the page. I have to stop every few paragraphs and wipe tears or take a controlled breath. It's not so much that the story is too sad. It's just that reading it in front of people is overwhelming. And there's this tremendous weight like my heart is being squeezed by my lungs. Think of a boa constrictor stuck in your chest.

But I notice with every page the weight lifts a little. Think of a boa constrictor letting go, wriggling away to find an easier meal.

Ever wonder if there are little cancer cells just growing

and multiplying inside of you? Ever wonder if you're stronger than they are?

That's what reading this story is like.

I look up and the circle of college kids is staring at me, jaws hanging open. None of them even knew I was in the army before today. All at once, in their eyes, there's understanding. Respect. Faith. One of them raises his hand.

"I just want to say," he starts, "that you gave me a whole different perspective on what's going on over there."

And I look to my professor. She nods her head and smiles at me. With her eyes she says, *I told you it was a good idea to read it out loud.*

As class dismisses, people stop to shake my hand. They thank me. These college students are actually grateful for what I did.

It's funny, but all I did besides sit in a dump truck during the ambush was write a story about it. It's funny, but the story is what matters. The story is what changes, at least for a moment, the way these people feel. And what an empowering sensation it is to share it.

After the semester ends, with my professor's encouragement, I begin writing about all the experiences I've had as a soldier. She helps me edit the pieces, send them to small journals for publication, and eventually, to organize them into a book.

Each piece I write I give to Heather. Then to my parents.

Slowly I feel comfortable talking about Iraq. And slowly, the more I talk about it, the more I realize that it's the words that save me.

They are only words, words we use every day. But they are the words of a heart, the silhouettes of a generation. They are *my* silhouettes. In between these words, there's the resilient silence of humanity. This is *my* silence.

////////////// **THE INNOCENT** //////////////

While I'm in college, I get a job at a before- and after-school program for kids. It's a perfect college job because the hours are in the morning and afternoon. I can go to class in between, get enough hours to afford my bills, and still have the nights and weekends. Not to mention we get paid for snow days.

Today we take a trip to the New York State Museum in Albany.

The ten children for whom I'm responsible are walking (single file, using inside voices) through the carpeted, snaking hallways.

We've passed the fake Iroquois Indians picking fake vegetables and warding off fake woolly mammoths. We've also walked through the woodland creatures exhibit. There, fake bobcats perch on a fake rock. And the rack from the fake moose epitomizes the grandeur of the Adirondack region. In another exhibit we've already passed fake ducks are split in half by a sheet of glass, apparently the surface of some imaginary lake.

We're in another exhibit now, a new exhibit, one that is anything but fake. But it's the only one I wish was. I wish I didn't understand this exhibit the way I do. I wish there wasn't a reason for this exhibit.

I wonder how in the world five years have passed already. How in the world did this crumpled piece of scrap metal go from iron ore in the ground to an I beam in a skyscraper to a display under glass in the New York State Museum?

This is my second time viewing this exhibit. I cried the first time I saw it, but today I have to retain my composure. I'm in charge of ten kids.

Leading kids is often like leading a platoon. I have to be sharp, decisive, and one step ahead. I have to be confident, admirable, and humble. I have to be respectful, compassionate, and disciplined. I have to be funny. I have to be strong. Or they'll walk all over me. So I don't cry.

I hold it in and supervise the kids as they roam around the room full of rusty bolts and torn airplane tires and a torched fire truck and quotes from George W. Bush and the American flag. It's *the* American flag, the flag that is tattered, stained, and outlined with frayed edges. But it's the flag, our flag, and it still flies, even if it's no longer watching over Manhattan.

The flag, like everything else in this room, seems to be smoking. The kids don't see the smoke. They are the innocent. But I see the smoke as if I'm running from it.

I'm reading a plaque that lies next to a smoking firefighter's helmet. It explains how the brave men and women of Engine such-and-such took such-and-such casualties. There's a word I hate: casualty. Why is it casual?

I stop reading because the smoke fills my eyes.

A little girl is standing next to me. Emma is in kindergarten this year. She's "one of the good ones." Her parents are funny and smart and friendly. They take the time to show Emma and her brother, Peter, the important things in life. Emma loves to tap-dance and go to Tae Kwon Do practice. She loves to color and to play kickball. She loves to laugh and dance and play dress-up. She is the innocent.

She looks up at me with giant brown eyes. She seems confused. There are other families here, walking among our field trip group, and they seem to choke on the smoke like I do. But Emma's not choking.

She looks at the yellow fireman's hat next to me and then at the flag. Then she looks back to me.

"What happened, Ryan?" she asks.

The way she says my name breaks my heart. It tears my

heart right in half, because I quickly do the math. Emma is barely five. She was born after the Towers fell.

Until now I considered these kids part of my generation. But they are not. My generation has already lost its innocence. I remember exactly when it happened, actually. The very day. The exact time is written right here, in fact, on plaques in the New York State Museum.

I wonder how I can retain Emma's innocence, how I can protect her generation. I cannot.

"Some very bad men attacked our country, Emma. Down in New York City," I say. "They don't like our country so they killed innocent people."

"But why?" she says. She looks around. "That doesn't make any sense."

"No, it doesn't," I say.

Then we stand for a minute, Emma contemplating how humans kill one another to prove points. Me still trying to figure that out myself.

"You know how the other kids talk about me being in Iraq, Emma?" I ask.

"Yeah," she says.

"This is why I went."

But really, if you ask me why I did it, why I volunteered, why I ran toward the danger when so many of my generation ran away, I'll rummage through an old army foot locker. I'll dig around between the handwritten letters and the Desert

Eagle flip knife. I'll move the Army Commendation Medal aside. I'll even dig past the folded American flag Heather would have gotten if I died.

Then I'll find Bazoona Cat.

I'll hold it for a moment, petting its soft fur, remembering the little boy who taught me Arabic. And then I'll place it in your hand.

You'll look at it with a curious sort of disgust. It is rather ugly. That's the first thing you'll notice. All its sentiment means nothing to you, and you'll hand it back like spoiled fruit.

I'll just smile because I know how much you can't understand, no matter how many words I use to describe it. But inside my heart will ache. I'll give up trying to explain the creature and just pet its soft fur.

You'll wonder how I can chalk up my involvement in the war to this hairy, gross little object. You'll wonder how I can justify everything that happened to me in Iraq with this stupid little rabbit's foot that resembles a cat. You'll wonder if I heard you right the first time.

"Why'd you do it?" you'll ask.

I'll hold up Bazoona Cat and say, "This is why."

////////// GHOSTS OF WAR //////////

It's not until I come home from combat that I realize what the drill sergeants were trying to tell us when they said, "There's no such thing as an atheist in a foxhole."

It's something so easy to write as words on paper, but it means nothing until you've seen it.

Without faith God is nothing, Allah is nothing, Buddha is nothing.

Without faith we are nothing.

Flying down a desert road from Kuwait to Iraq, I watch humanity's evil in the form of children begging for food. Sitting in a dump truck in downtown Samarra, I see evil littering the sky with pieces of children. Walking to chow in Abu Ghraib, it's airburst mortars; flying down a torn-up dirt road, it's fake explosives. As I salvage parts from a Humvee or stand for taps at Joe Nurre's funeral or stand in front of a fence at Ground Zero, I cannot escape it.

I am human. I am evil. But I am also beautiful. I can do great things, but I can do evil things. I can save myself. And I can save the world.

"There's no such thing as an atheist in a foxhole."

I never once stand in a foxhole in Iraq. But I see people die, I know of people's deaths, and I understand that it's something caused by the hand of another human being. I don't know if I'll be alive tomorrow.

All I know is that humanity's evil exists. I know of humanity's beauty. And the only thing of which I can be sure is that there is something more.

The bullets fly, the mortars fall, people die, evil triumphs, and it is all somehow beautiful. Not on the surface. It's ugly at face value. It's terrifying and horribly ugly.

But underneath and between the lines, that's where it's glorious. It's magnificent and perfect there, this place that has no words, this place that is beyond. This place where things are more than they seem but cost less than they're worth.

This place is beautiful. This place is war.

War has been glorified in our culture, and for so long I assumed it was a sick obsession with death and evil. After seeing war, after experiencing it, I know how much deeper it goes.

War is hell, but war is also paradise. War encompasses all that we are, all that we were, and all that we will be. I look at war, my war, and I see past the blood and guts and bullets and bombs.

I see the soft things that hide inside the casings of bullets. I see the hint of light at the top of a mushroom cloud. I see the devils inside the dust. I see the hunters being hunted. And the moon dancing on waves, the sun dancing on dust.

I see the ghosts of war.

I see the message. And that message astounds me, because, even though I celebrate Christmas, and even though I study Zen philosophy, and even though I see countless Muslims place their mats and pray toward Mecca, in war, in a foxhole, my epiphany is when I realize that there is something out there bigger than myself.

It's not about believing. It's not about ideas or who's right and who's wrong. It's just sudden. It just exists.

There is something more.

And now I see that I am grateful for war, for the ghosts. I'm grateful for the worst in humanity, because it's the closest I'll ever get to understanding the best in humanity. I'm grateful for my moments of insanity, because it's the closest I'll ever get to becoming sane.

It's a lot like love. You can tell a thousand love stories, but only those who've been in love will truly understand what it is you're talking about. Even when you are in love, it's impossible to understand. But that's the way love has to be. That's the way war has to be.

And when the war is over, I'm sitting at home one day, and I miss it.

I miss the power, and I miss the vulnerability. I miss the innocence, and I miss the guilt. I miss the death, and I miss the life.

I long for it, but I know it can't come back. So I hold on to it.

We call this faith.

And without faith we are nothing.

201 file: The repository of all personnel records for an individual service member.

50 cal. (Browning .50 caliber): A heavy machine gun also known as the M2 and "Ma Deuce."

550 cord: Lightweight nylon kernmantle rope.

AAR (After Action Review): An assessment conducted after a mission or training exercise to discover what happened, why it happened, and how to improve for next time.

Abu Ghraib prison: Originally known as the prison where Saddam Hussein's government tortured and executed dissidents or those who spoke out against his government. In 2004, Abu Ghraib became associated with a prisoner abuse scandal when it was discovered that U.S. soldiers had tortured and humiliated Iraqi detainees.

ACE (Ammo, Casualties, Equipment) report: A check on

the amount of ammo, the condition of any casualties, and the status of equipment.

Active Duty: Full-time service in the armed forces.

ACU (Army Combat Uniform): The most recent uniform of the U.S. Army.

A-driver (Assistant driver): A soldier sitting in the passenger seat of a vehicle in a convoy, responsible for manning the radio and assisting the driver in general awareness.

AIT (Advanced Individual Training): Training soldiers receive in their chosen MOS.

AK-47: A 7.62 mm assault rifle. Due to its durability and ease of use, it is the most widely used assault rifle in the world.

ASVAB (Armed Services Vocational Aptitude Battery): A multiple-choice test used to determine one's qualification for enlistment in the armed forces.

AT (Annual Training): Two-week training reservists must conduct every year of their enlistment.

AT4: A portable one-shot antitank weapon used more commonly today to destroy or disable armored vehicles and fortifications; its name is a pun on the weapon's caliber of 84 mm.

AWOL (Absent Without Leave): To be absent from post without a valid pass or leave.

Battalion: A military unit of about 500–1,500 soldiers, usually consisting of between two and seven companies and typically commanded by a lieutenant colonel.

BCT (Basic Combat Training): Nine-week training that every soldier must complete upon enlistment; does not include the week of in-processing called reception.

Berm: Pile of dirt usually used as a perimeter defense.

Blackwater: Blackwater Worldwide (formerly Blackwater USA); a private military contractor used mostly for security services in Iraq.

Blue Phase: The last three weeks of BCT, signified by a blue guidon.

Bobcat: A brand of skid steer loader used for small construction jobs.

BRASS (Breathe, Relax, Aim, Sight picture, Squeeze): Acronym for the proper shooting technique.

BRM (Basic Rifle Marksmanship): Rifle practice and qualification that every soldier must complete in basic training and must remain proficient in throughout his or her career.

Buck Sergeant: Jargon for pay grade E-5, or the first rank of sergeant.

C130: A tactical four-engine turboprop military transport aircraft.

Cadence: A chant sung by military personnel while parading or marching to stay in step.

Chain of Command: A bureaucratic system in which each employee answers to only one supervisor.

Chinook: A twin-engine, tandem rotor, heavy-lift helicopter.

CID (Criminal Investigation Division): The federal law enforcement agency that investigates serious crimes and violations of civilian and military law.

Company: A military unit of about 75–200 soldiers, usually consisting of between three and five platoons and typically commanded by a captain.

CQ (Command Quarters): A building or other structure from which company-level decisions are made; also known as a

TOC (Tactical Operations Center).

Cross-level: A process by which the army transfers soldiers between units, dictated by deployment circumstances.

CS gas (2-chlorobenzalmalononitrile): Tear gas.

DCU (Desert Camouflage Uniform): The brown-and-tan uniform used by the U.S. Army in desert operations. Use of this uniform discontinued in October 2007.

DFAC (Dining Facility): A chow hall where soldiers eat.

DoD (Department of Defense): The U.S. government agency that overseas all functions related to national security and the military.

Double Time: Jargon for "run."

ECP (Entry Control Point): Controlled entrance to an army post, camp, or FOB.

EOD (Explosive Ordinance Disposal): A team of soldiers who render safe the hazardous or explosive devices encountered by the military.

ETD (Estimated Time of Departure): Leaving times for a flight or convoy.

E-Tool (Entrenching tool): Collapsible shovel.

FOB (Forward Operations Base): Any secured forward position that is used to support tactical operations.

Formation: Gathering of soldiers by rank and file, used for accountability and marching.

Front leaning rest position: Push-up position.

FTX (Field Training Exercise): An exercise during which soldiers train as if they are at war.

Full battle rattle: Jargon for "fully geared"; consists of Kevlar (helmet), body armor, rifle, and ammunition.

Geneva Convention: Four treaties formulated in Geneva, Switzerland, from 1864–1949 that set the standard for the rules of war, including the rules of engagement and the treatment of noncombatants and prisoners of war.

Guidon: A flag that companies or platoons carry to signify their unit designation or corps affiliation.

Haji: A Muslim who has made the hajj, or pilgrimage to Mecca, one of the five pillars, or obligations, of Islam. Soldiers of the Iraq War use "haji" in both a derogatory manner and in a general way to describe something Middle Eastern or Muslim.

Halliburton: One of the world's largest providers of products and services to the energy industry.

HEMTT (Heavy Expanded Mobile Tactical Truck): A range of 8x8 diesel-powered, off-road capable trucks. A 10x10 variant of the HEMTT is used as prime mover in the Palletized Load System (PLS).

Herringbone: Staggered formation in which every vehicle of a convoy is a certain distance apart on alternate sides of the road.

Hesco barriers: Large bastions for perimeter defense and usually filled by scoop loaders.

HMMWV (Highly Mobile Multipurpose Wheeled Vehicle): Diesel-powered trucks used for carrying personnel and light cargo, "Humvees" have been the military's vehicle of choice since 1979.

Hy-ex (Hydraulic Excavator): A track-mounted, hydraulic-controlled vehicle used for excavating earth, rock, sand, and for moving construction materials.

IED (Improvised Explosive Device): A homemade

explosive device used in unconventional warfare and the leading cause of U.S./Coalition casualties in Operations Iraqi Freedom and Enduring Freedom.

Insurgent: Participant of a violent uprising against a government.

Kalashnikov: See AK-47.

KBR (Kellogg, Brown and Root): An American engineering and construction company that provides logistical support to U.S. and Coalition forces in Operations Iraqi Freedom and Enduring Freedom.

Kevlar: A light, strong synthetic fiber used by the military mostly in body armor and ballistic helmets, the latter now referred to as Kevlar.

Logistics: The management of the flow of goods, information, or other services from the point of origin to the point of consumption.

LOGPAC (Logistics Package): A convoy used for logistics purposes.

Lower enlisted: Soldiers below pay grade E-5. From lowest to highest rank: private (E-1), private (E-2), private first class (E-3), specialist (E-4), and corporal (E-4).

M16: A semiautomatic rifle that fires 5.56 mm rounds, the standard weapon issued to the U.S. soldier.

M203: A single-shot 40 mm grenade launcher that attaches to the M16.

M60: An American general-purpose machine gun that fires 7.62 mm rounds.

M916: A tractor truck used by the military to haul various cargo.

M978: See HEMMT.

MEDEVAC (Medical Evacuation): The timely and efficient removal of soldiers from the battlefield via aircraft or ambulance so that they may receive urgent medical attention.

MEPS (Military Entrance Processing Station): Location where entrants and applicants are processed for military service.

Mobilization training: The first stage of a modern deployment wherein soldiers train before being shipped overseas.

Mortar: A muzzle-loaded weapon that launches a low-velocity explosive shell and is used for indirect, short-range fire.

MOS (Military Occupational Specialty): Job classification of military personnel.

MP (Military Police): The police of a military organization. In Iraq, the MP's main missions include area security, usually by vehicle patrol, and the capture and supervision of prisoners of war and other detainees.

MRE (Meal, Ready to Eat): A self-contained, individual field ration.

MSR (Main Service Route): A route designated within an area of operations upon which the bulk of traffic flows in support of military operations.

National Guard: A reserve military force funded by the state in which the units reside.

NCO (Noncommissioned Officer): An enlisted rank defined by its leadership responsibility; includes all the grades of sergeant.

OD (Olive Drab): A very ugly shade of green.

OPFOR (Opposing Force): A military unit designated as the enemy in a war training scenario.

OPSEC (Operational Security): A methodology of keeping secret information from the enemy.

Parade rest: A more relaxed position of attention used in formation and when talking to noncommissioned officers. Head and eyes forward, back straight, shoulders back, hands clasped behind the back, feet shoulder-width apart.

PAX terminal: A structure in which passengers wait for aircraft.

Phonetic alphabet: A system in which a code word is assigned to each letter of the English alphabet, used for clarification purposes over a radio.

Platoon: A military unit of about 30–50 soldiers, usually consisting of between two to four squads and typically commanded by a lieutenant.

PLS (Palletized Load System): A logistics supply program used in conjunction with the HEMTT.

PMCS (Preventative Maintenance Checks and Services): The checks, service, and maintenance performed before, during, and after any movement.

Position of attention: A strict form used in formation and when talking to commissioned officers. Head and eyes forward, back straight, each thumb curled so that it touches the first joint of each forefinger, each hand straight along the seams of the trousers, heels touch so the feet form a 45-degree angle.

Prone position: The position of the body lying facedown.

PT (Physical Training): Military exercise programs.

PTSD (Posttraumatic Stress Disorder): Anxiety disorder that can develop from exposure to one or more traumatic events.

PX (Post Exchange): Store operated by the Army and Air Force Exchange Program.

QRF (Quick Reaction Force): A military unit, usually cavalry, that is poised to respond on very short notice, typically less than fifteen minutes.

Q-West (Qayyarah West): An airbase in Iraq approximately 300 kilometers north of Baghdad.

Reception: A weeklong system for in-processing recruits before they begin BCT.

Red Phase: The first three weeks of BCT, signified by a red guidon.

Reserves: A reserve military force funded by the federal government.

RPG (Rocket Propelled Grenade): A shoulder-launched antitank weapon used by the Iraqi insurgency.

Rucksack: Standard issue backpack used by soldiers to carry supplies.

SAW (Squad Automatic Weapon): A one-man machine gun that fires 5.56 mm rounds.

Sector of fire: A defined area that is required to be covered by the fire of a weapon-carrying individual or crew.

SF (Special Forces): Highly trained military units that conduct specialized operations, such as reconnaissance, unconventional warfare, or counterterrorism actions.

Sheik: "Elder," in Arabic; used to denote the elder of a tribe, a lord, a revered wise man, or an Islamic scholar

SINCGARS (Single Channel Ground and Airborne Radio System): A reliable, secure, and easily maintained radio.

Smart Book: Slang for the CTT (Common Tasks and Training) manual issued to recruits in BCT.

SOP (Standard Operating Procedure): Set of guidelines to perform a given operation or in response to a given event.

Squad: A small military unit led by an NCO.

TA50: Field clothing and equipment.

Third country national: An individual of another nationality hired by a government or a government-sanctioned contractor who represent neither the contracting government nor the host country or area of operations.

UA (Unit Administrator): Soldier or civilian of a unit responsible for written communications, including memorandums, messages, reports, plans, forms, briefings, alert rosters, and miscellaneous correspondence.

VFW (Veterans of Foreign Wars): A congressionally chartered war veterans organization open to current members of the U.S. military or those who have received an honorable discharge.

White Phase: The second three weeks of BCT, signified by a white guidon.

///////// ACKNOWLEDGMENTS /////////

A
lthough this book is a personal account of one individual, by no means could it have been accomplished without the willed efforts of so many selfless people.

First and foremost, I would like to thank my family and extended family who continue to enthusiastically support my writing and accomplishments. An entire book has been written in honor of my wife, Heather, and her sacrifices; they have allowed me to continue pursuing my dreams. Thank you, Heather, for never giving up, for forgiving me when I couldn't even begin to forgive myself, and for making me a better man. Thank you Mom and Dad, for your unparalleled belief in me since, well, birth. I wouldn't be the man I am today without your unconditional love and insightful guidance to support me along the way.

Thank you to my sister, Regan, for your understanding and for always looking up to me, even when you probably shouldn't have.

Secondly, to the people whom I've met along the road who have changed the very nature of that road: Thank you Maria Pollack and family for helping me develop my "therapy" into something more than just words on paper. Thank you to my agent, Jodie Rhodes, for your stroke of genius and to the HarperCollins team of editors, especially Phoebe Yeh and Greg Ferguson, for their expertise and for allowing me to share my generation's story. Thank you to my coach, Jim McHugh, for seeing potential from the very first takedown. Thank you to my childhood teacher, Tammy Warren, for always challenging me to be more creative. And thank you to all the kids at GCC for being innocent.

Finally, a special thank you to Andy Zeltwanger; your bravery, wisdom, and guidance saved us more times and in more ways than I'll ever know. And to all the members of EQ platoon: I never will forget your tremendous sacrifices and courage in the face of an evil we couldn't possibly understand. Thank you for your service and for the amazing impact you've had on my life.

General George Patton once said, "Freedom has a taste, and for those who have fought for it the taste is so sweet, the protected will never know." Thank you, James Conklin, and all soldiers past, present, and future who tasted freedom.